About the Author

Jerry Wyant, BSBA Economics University of Missouri

Author of "Basic Economics for Students and Non-Students Alike", available for FREE download in e-book format and available for purchase in paperback format:

https://www.smashwords.com/profile/view/eotjerry

http://www.amazon.com/dp/B00C8UX2LO/ref=r_soa_s_i

Website of Basic Concepts in Economics:
http://www.economicsonlinetutor.com

Author's Facebook Page:
https://www.facebook.com/jerry.wyant

"Economics Online Tutor" Facebook page:
http://www.facebook.com/economicsonlinetutor

"Making Education Work" Facebook page:
http://www.facebook.com/MakingEducationWork

Home: Creston, Iowa

Family: wife Linda, daughter Lillie

Sanity and Public Policy:

Separating Truth from Truisms

By Jerry Wyant

Table of Contents

Just the Facts

How long do you have to ignore facts before they go away?

Well, actually, they never will go away. About the best you can do is to isolate yourself from them. You can quit listening to the people who keep bringing them up. Instead, you can just listen to others who want to ignore those pesky things. You can live in a world where the facts don't exist. That should help to reinforce your positions.

Or perhaps there is a better way: you can create an alternative set of facts, ones that you are more comfortable with. Make up an alternative reality; rewrite history. This way, you can find more people who agree with you. Take these alternative facts, put them in simplistic lingo that appeals to people's basic instincts, and there you have it!

Simplicity is the way to go. Replace facts with slogans; the truth with truisms. People don't want to be bothered with deep thoughts in order to form opinions. Provide them with an easier alternative, and they won't have to go to the trouble of thinking for themselves. Once people have heard a truism, they won't question whether the truism is the actual truth. You can even convince people that they are actually thinking for themselves, if you make that one of the truisms. Not only will you get many people who agree with you, but you can also deepen their convictions. Just insult anybody who dares to question your truisms. Tell your listeners that your position is the only true one, and that everybody who disagrees with you is lying. You don't necessarily need to ignore these naysayers, because you have ready-made arguments to counter what they say. Just respond to whatever kinds of facts or logic that they use with your slogans. Don't try to follow their logic, point by point.

That might create doubt in your mind; you wouldn't want that. Your mind is already made up and nobody is going to change it! When people argue with logic and facts, just change the subject back to the simplistic lingo. It helps to have a truism prepared to demonize those who use logic. Just use words like "elitism" a lot. The people you are really trying to reach won't be swayed by mere logic and reality, anyway. Rationality - who needs it?

Simplicity is the way to go.

The best way to make this alternative reality gain support: repetition. The truisms become talking points. The more often people hear simplistic truisms the more deeply they will agree with them. If people hear the same things often enough, things that ring true because they appeal to their basic instincts, the less likely they are to question them. Don't let the discussion veer away from your talking points. Stay on track. Just keep repeating your talking points. Voila! This alternative reality becomes THE reality!

Of course, the underlying truths, the ones that exist in the real world, will not go away. Facts are facts. This means that the process of inventing alternative truths is an ongoing process. You will have to be continuously creating new facts to explain away any real world events or results that don't jive with your version of reality.

But this is easy to do because you have a system in place that makes creating alternative facts relatively easy.

The Invisible Hand

According to classical economic theory, the cumulative effect of buyers and sellers acting in their own self-interest will benefit society by creating the most efficient outcome of market price and quantity. The "invisible hand" is the idea that something as beneficial as maximum market efficiency can be the result of countless decisions being made in self-interest.

The concept is rather simple. In all markets, whether we are talking about product markets, labor markets, or something else, buyers want to receive the "most" or "best" but pay the least. That is the self-interest motive from the buyers' side. Sellers, on the other hand, want to maximize profits. Profits are defined as revenue minus costs, so sellers want to conduct business in a manner that maximizes the amount that revenue exceeds costs. Sellers look towards getting the highest prices at the lowest cost. That is the self-interest motive from the sellers' side.

The interests of the buyers and sellers are conflicting interests. The give-and-take of market forces creates equilibrium between these conflicting interests, and the maximum-efficiency economic outcome is the result of this give-and-take.

In this scenario, market efficiency is the result of the give-and-take of market forces unleashed by two sides of transactions acting in their own self-interest. There is an important lesson to learn here:

The self-interest of buyers does not create efficient markets.

The self-interest of sellers does not create efficient markets.

Only the give-and-take between the two opposing self-interests creates efficient markets.

Market efficiency can only result if both sides have equal market power. In this theory, there is no way to achieve market efficiency without each side being equal in market power.

Policies that give one side of this equation more market power than the other side do not promote market efficiency. These policies do the exact opposite; they promote inefficiency. The idea that somehow better results will occur if we have a set of policies that favors one side or the other is a fallacious idea.

The idea that better results will occur if we have no policies, or fewer policies, because doing so will "get the government out of the way and let the free market work its magic" is also fallacious, unless it can be shown that doing so would promote equal market power between buyers and sellers. Such a result would be very difficult to show. Except for the extreme situation of pure anarchy, the government by its very existence creates the conditions in which a market economy functions. Without anarchy, there is going to be government involvement. It isn't government involvement per se that creates inefficient markets; it is unequal footing between buyers and sellers that does so. "No policy" is a policy.

The invisible hand is a theory from a simplified version of a more complex real world. Even so, this theory is used to justify policies designed to give more market power to sellers at the expense of buyers in the product markets, and more power to buyers at the expense of sellers in the labor markets. This is being done in the name of market efficiency.

Such policies do not follow rationally from the theory that is being used for their justification.

Free Market Pricing

(Basic Economics Explained in Everyday Language)

Everything has a cost. There simply is not enough of everything to satisfy all of the wants and needs that exist in the world. In other words, the world does not contain an endless supply of everything. Consumers must choose among all of their available options in order to decide what to do with their limited budgets. Producers (businesses) must consider what consumers want and the costs of their resources to determine what, and how much, to produce.

The next three (short) paragraphs include the basic theory of free markets. If you only read that far, you will come away with a basic understanding of the theory of the free market system (capitalism). If you read through to the end, you will come away with a basic understanding of some of the differences between the theory and real-world applications, as well as the some of the important differences between capitalism and socialism.

Consumers will tend to purchase more of something if the cost of that something decreases relative to their other options. Producers will tend to produce more of something if they can receive a higher price for selling, within the framework of their cost structure. Consumers will use their budgets in such a way as to get as much satisfaction as possible; producers will determine what to sell in such a way as to maximize their profits.

Since consumers want to pay the smallest price possible and producers want to sell for the highest price possible, the amount that actually gets traded would be the quantity where the price that consumers are willing and able to pay matches the price that produces are willing and able to sell for. This is the basic concept of the free market system: demand equals supply. The price that equates demand with supply is the equilibrium, or market, price.

The beauty of this system is in its efficiency. Everything is done voluntarily. Each party to each transaction is entering into it voluntarily. Whoever decides to opt out voluntarily does so. If the price is too high for a particular consumer, that consumer will simply choose not to participate in that particular market, and use the budget for something else. If the price is too low, then it won't get produced. Only when the demand and supply are equal will the resources of both consumers and producers be used efficiently.

The major drawback for a socialist system is that resources will not be used efficiently, resulting in an inefficient amount of goods and services being produced. Efficient markets require that all costs be factored into the voluntary decisions to buy and sell. But by definition, a socialist system includes costs that cannot be accurately calculated. By definition, a socialist system is one in which the government owns some or all of the factors of production: the land where the production takes place, including the natural resources on the land; the equipment, machinery, and raw materials that have been previously produced but are used in the production process; the labor of the employees. All of these have costs because there are many options for their use. While the resources are being used for a specific activity, they are not available to be used for a different activity. Whatever value is placed on the best alternative activity, then, becomes the true cost of the use of resources. Determining whether they are getting put to use most efficiently requires knowing what their costs are. In a market (capitalist) economy, each of these resources has its own market to determine their efficient price. In a socialist economy, some or all of these resources will not have a market to determine their efficient price. Instead, the government sets the price or provides the resources for "free". For the overall economy to optimize its growth potential, for maximizing the standard of living for the population, efficient production and pricing is necessary. That is why you will tend to see that economic systems that are mostly capitalistic tend to have higher long-term economic growth, with more consumer choices and higher standards of living, than mostly socialistic economic systems.

Perhaps you already understand all of this. Perhaps that means that you know more about economics than you thought you did. This truth is somewhat paradoxical, however. The above explanation makes sense, but what it doesn't say is that it is all based on certain assumptions. The explanation is theoretical; the real world does not provide a perfect match for the theory. Often, people who take economics classes forget about the underlying assumptions and end up drawing the wrong conclusions. Many people draw conclusions based on the outcome of a theoretical model for perfectly free markets; but perfectly free markets do not exist in the real world. Economists use assumptions in order to isolate specific relationships to study, but when those relationships are applied to the real world the isolating assumptions have to be lifted. That is where the complexity of the study of economics comes into play: knowing what the assumptions are, what makes them unrealistic, and understanding the different relationships that are changed because the assumptions are not realistic. The study of economics involves many different concepts. Understanding the basics of each of these would be required in order to have a full understanding of how different economic activities are inter-related.

Here is a tip that might help you to decide if your conclusions regarding economic issues and economic policy are based on the real-world application of economic principles or are instead based on unrealistic assumptions from theory: Can you explain both why and how a particular policy or economic relationship, the actual process, leads to your personal conclusions? Have you thought through the process of how things work, who would be affected, what the likely outcomes would be, without the need to cite some theory? If so, you are on the right track. But if the reasoning behind your position is along the lines of "that's how the system works" or "this is the best solution because economic theory says so, and therefore I won't consider any alternatives", without having anything more substantive to back up your position, then you are likely basing your arguments on unrealistic assumptions.

Free markets may not exist in their purest form, but there are varying degrees of them. Generalizations, then, can be made based on concepts like "mostly free" or "mostly not free" markets. That means that the concept of free markets can be discussed in real-world terms.

"Market failure" is a broad term used to describe situations where the free market system creates drawbacks; in fact it creates inefficiencies instead of efficient markets. Often, market failure results from free markets not being "purely" free markets after the assumptions are lifted. Purely free markets require every party to every transaction to have the exact same information at their disposal for making decisions, as long as the information is relevant to that decision. Purely free markets require all of the factor markets (labor, land, capital) also to be purely free. These requirements, and more, do not hold true in the real world; the real world contains no purely free markets.

Another important point involves the difference between the real world of economics and the political rhetoric. I mentioned above that "economic systems that are mostly capitalistic tend to have higher long-term economic growth, with more consumer choices and higher standards of living, than mostly socialistic economic systems". This is true, based on economic principles as well as world history. However, it holds true because socialism is a system of government or collective ownership of the factors of production (land, labor, capital). The rhetoric that any government involvement equates to socialism does not fit the definition, and does not fit the real world conclusions about growth, choices, and the standard of living. If the government doesn't control the resources, it isn't socialism.

The idea that any government involvement equates to socialism not only uses an incorrect definition of socialism, it also uses faulty logic. A government is at the very heart of an organized society; without government, the market system as we know it could not exist. Instead, we would have pure anarchy, a system in which the strongest have the ability and a motive to destroy everybody else economically. In short, the government by its very existence creates every type of economic system other than pure anarchy. The government's existence allows the businesses to exist, and provides customers for the businesses. It makes no sense at all to automatically assume that every perceived or real problem can be solved simply by eliminating the government from the equation. The level of government involvement could indeed create problems, but it could also eliminate problems. Remember, free markets do not exist in the real world. Each situation should be analyzed separately with no preconceived notion that government is always "bad" (or always "good").

I would like to briefly mention a couple of specific areas where free markets often are not allowed to exist in today's world. Both of these topics are controversial. I won't go into all of the controversy, but I do want to mention that both valid and invalid arguments have been publicly presented to argue for or against specific aspects of these areas. The more you understand about economics, the more you will be able to use valid arguments to support your personal positions on controversial issues. At the same time, the more you understand about economics, the more you will realize that the "other side" of the issues may also have valid points to make. Political arguments over policy tend to be based on rhetoric, half-truths, and misleading information; much more so than being based on thorough cost and benefit analysis using only truthful statements. Because of this, the arguments tend to be invalid.

The first controversial area that I want to mention is the minimum wage. A minimum wage is a kind of price control, taking the price away from being totally set by market forces of supply and demand. There are two kinds of controversies involved with a minimum wage: whether to have one at all; and if so, at what level to set it. I won't go into those controversies (doing so would involve a very lengthy discussion that is off-topic for the purpose of this writing), but they involve real or perceived market failures. I just want to mention how minimum wages affect supply and demand in the market; in this case, the market for labor. In the labor market, a free market will set the price (wage rate) at the level where the demand (the number of workers that employers want to hire) is equal to the supply (the number of potential employees, or people offering their labor services). A minimum wage will set a floor price that the wage rate can go to. If the minimum wage is below the market wage, then the market will not be affected. The market wage will prevail. But if the minimum wage is set above the market wage, then the market wage will NOT prevail. The price will be set above the market price, at the minimum wage. Since a higher wage means a higher amount of labor supplied and a lower amount of labor demanded, more potential workers will want jobs at that wage rate. But employers will want to hire fewer workers at that wage rate. The result: more people will want jobs than the amount of jobs available, resulting in unemployment. You probably have heard people say that the minimum wage hurts unskilled workers because it creates unemployment. This is what they are talking about. However - be careful about making the wrong assumptions about this. Part of the unemployment is because employers will hire fewer workers than what a free market price would produce. The people who lose their jobs for this reason will be "hurt" by the minimum wage. But the other part of the unemployment doesn't hurt any workers: the part where more people want to work only because the wages are higher. They wouldn't have jobs even at the free market wage; they simply add their names to the pool of potential workers. They get reclassified to unemployed, where before they were classified as not in the labor force at all. This is an area of economics that has been studied extensively, and studies tend to show that the rhetoric overstates the number of people who actually lose jobs due to a minimum wage. The reason behind this reality involves the various choices that employers have available in order to deal with a minimum wage, as well as the elasticity in both the labor and the product markets. Elasticity is an important concept in the study of economics. The topic of elasticity cannot be explained within the framework of this writing. I encourage everybody to at least familiarize themselves with the basic principles involved; check the "further reading" suggestions below.

The other area where free markets do not exist that I want to mention is the area of health care. Obviously, with high costs and politically-charged opinions dominating the news, this is a very controversial issue, and I don't want to get into the controversy here. The politics behind the arguments over Obamacare is a topic that requires its own analysis, outside the purpose of this writing; so is the real-world problem of healthcare costs. I am specifically mentioning healthcare as a topic only to relate it to free market supply and demand, and why the free market does not always prevail (regardless of any personal beliefs). Remember that in a free market, the price is set at the amount produced where demand equals supply. This only works in a free market when people voluntarily take themselves out of the market because of the price. In free markets, people are free to choose whether to, and how much to, participate in any given market, and when to use their limited resources for some other purpose. Those with the most resources will have the most choices; those with no resources available will not be able to participate in a market at all. If they can't afford something, they won't buy it. For health care, this would mean that people who cannot afford health care do not get health care. It means that the resulting supply of health care workers, and the amount and quality of health care research will be based on price, not on any other consideration. The other considerations to take into account would include such things as: life expectancy; healthy workers to keep the economy growing and increase the standard of living for everybody; reducing the number of disabled people in society; the idea of letting people die or suffer simply because of their personal financial situation, even if the technology and national wealth exist to prevent these problems. All of these concepts, and more, would not be taken into consideration if health care was left entirely up to the free market system. Just as importantly, all of these involve externalities, which are costs and benefits to society can be easily identified but not factored into any market price or quantity.

The study of economics is divided into two broad categories: microeconomics and macroeconomics. Microeconomics is the study of economics on an individual basis: the individual business, the individual worker, the individual consumer - that sort of thing. Macroeconomics is the study of the overall economy: a nation's total output, unemployment, inflation, globalization, taxation, government spending, monetary policy.

Further reading

For more information on specific topics within the study of economics that are mentioned in this essay:

BASIC ECONOMICS FOR STUDENTS AND NON-STUDENTS ALIKE by Jerry Wyant

Available for purchase as a paperback or free download in e-book format at Amazon, Barnes & Noble, Apple, Sony, Smashwords, and other distributors. The same information is available at my free website:

www.economicsonlinetutor.com

Let's Connect the Dots

The economy sucks. Agreed?

Agreed.

Now that we are on the same page, let's take a closer look at this problem.

If the economy is so bad, who among us is really hurting?

Everybody.

You say everybody is hurting? How are the giant multi-national corporations doing?

Actually, they are doing quite well. Profits are near record levels; they have more cash than they know how to spend.

If the economy sucks, that means that Wall Street is tanking, right?

No, Wall Street is doing quite well also.

Then, who is hurting? The wealth of the richest among us must be wiped out, right?

No, the rich keep getting richer and richer.

Then who is it that is hurting, if the economy is really that bad?

Just about everybody else. Except for those giant corporations, Wall Street, and super rich individuals, everybody else is feeling the pinch. Very few jobs are available. Long term unemployment is high. Those with jobs receive low wages with fewer benefits. Poverty is high and growing. There doesn't seem to be any money to help grow our small businesses, so they suffer along with us. The middle class is shrinking before our eyes.

In that case, what should we do about it?

Well, let's connect the dots. Big corporations, Wall Street, super rich individuals doing great while everybody else is hurting.

Why in the world would anybody think that under these conditions, giving more breaks to those who are doing great, and making everybody else who is already hurting pay for these breaks, will fix this kind of problem?

Wise up, everybody!

Job Creators, Taxes and Inequality

"Corporations are job creators."

"We would have more jobs if taxes on the rich were lower."

"Taxing the rich takes money away from those who earn it."

"Corporations would create more jobs if the government would let them keep more of their money."

"The reason why the economy is hurting is because of oppressive taxes on the rich and on corporations."

"Progressive taxes and welfare are socialist wealth redistributions that destroy the economy."

"If you raise taxes on job creators, it will destroy the economy".

We hear such statements ad nauseam. Surely they must be true if everybody is saying so, right? Even raising revenue for the government by closing tax loopholes for the wealthiest is considered heresy. If we close these loopholes, it amounts to "raising taxes on job creators". What are the merits of such claims? Would raising taxes on the rich be a job-killer, because that is what happens when you tax "job creators"?

The first question to ask is this: are rich corporations and individuals really job creators? For the sake of argument, let's just assume for now that they are. So, will raising taxes on these job creators really kill jobs?

Let's think through the process of how this all works. Instead of relying on some vague theory, or political rhetoric, think through the actual process. First of all, income taxes, whatever the rates, only apply to pretax gains. The original investment is not taxed, only the gains. For any given income tax rate, people can use their BEFORE-TAX income on something that can be written off on their tax return, thus reducing their taxes, or they can use this income on something that WON'T reduce their taxes. In that case, they will be paying taxes at the marginal rate on that income. If they hire workers, and therefore "create jobs", then the salaries and benefits that they pay out to workers become business expenses. They won't pay taxes on this money because it is deducted from revenue before computing taxable income. If they decide not to hire workers, and keep the money as profits, then they WILL have to pay taxes on this money. Unless they find somewhere else to invest the money, an investment in something that does NOT create jobs, they will have to pay taxes on this money. But if they hire workers with the money, then they won't have to pay taxes on it. That is how the tax code works. Hire workers, pay fewer taxes. Don't hire workers, and either pay more taxes or invest in something other than job creation.

To repeat: for any given tax rate, hire workers and pay fewer taxes. Don't hire workers, and either pay more taxes or invest in something that doesn't create jobs.

That is what happens for any given tax rate. What happens when the tax rate changes?

If you increase the tax rates on these job creators, then the tax that they pay on everything EXCEPT jobs will go up. They still won't have to pay taxes on the money that they spend for employee compensation. A tax increase will give them an incentive to invest in the business, because it is the cost of NOT investing that goes up. The cost of investing does not increase. An increase in the income tax rate won't give them an incentive NOT to invest in job creation. This will not be an incentive for killing jobs; it will be an incentive for creating jobs. Job creation takes money out of the column that is taxable and puts it in the column that is not taxable. This is simple mathematics; not political rhetoric, but mathematics.

If you decrease the tax rates on these job creators, then there will be no added incentive to create jobs. The amount of income taxes paid on employee salaries and benefits for these job creators is zero either way. What a tax rate decrease does is decrease the taxes that they have to pay on the money that they aren't using to create jobs anyway. The cost of paying for jobs does not go up, but the cost of NOT creating jobs goes down. It is an incentive for them to keep more profits that are taxable. It is in no way an incentive for them to spend the money on job creation; again, mathematics and not rhetoric.

Please re-read from the beginning if you don't understand this concept so far. This is a concept that is important to our economy today. It explains to a large degree how we have been spending so much time struggling through a "jobless recovery" even as large corporations are reporting record profits and record cash levels. These corporations already have more cash than they are investing back into their businesses. Interest rates for them to finance job creation through borrowing are at historical lows, near zero. Yet they aren't investing this money on jobs. The wealthiest individuals have recovered from the recession while the incomes of everybody else have fallen, increasing the already-wide wealth gap. With this amount of cash and job-creating ability already, why do we have so many unemployed people? The political rhetoric is that these job creators just need one more benefit from us, on top of their record cash reserves, in the form of lower taxes, in order for them to have an incentive to create jobs. Or that the millions of unemployed Americans are all lazy anyway. Or that somehow, these workers aren't qualified to take back the jobs that they were laid off from.

That is the political rhetoric. The reality is something different entirely. The reality is that: (1) raising taxes on the rich doesn't kill jobs, and lowering taxes on the rich doesn't create jobs, as explained above; and (2) the rich are not the real job creators, as explained below.

For the above explanation about taxes, I left in the assumption that the rich are the ones that create jobs in order to focus on the effects of tax rates for the richest Americans. But the truth is that consumers are the ones that create jobs. Tax rates for the rich have nothing to do with it. If a business of any size sees a way to increase before-tax profits, it would be to their advantage to do so. They want to keep their tax bills at a minimum, of course, but raising before-tax profits will also raise after-tax profits. Very little money for rich individuals and for corporations will be caught up in the margin where the additional before-tax profits will be lower than the additional taxes. If any business decision-makers worry about the taxes more than the actual effects on the bottom line, then they aren't making wise decisions. Increasing before-tax profits for all practical purposes is the same thing as increasing after-tax profits.

If businesses or potential businesses see a demand for their products and/or services that will generate a profit, they will do what they can to get that profit. If it means hiring more workers in order to meet that demand, and the cost of additional workers is lower than the addition to potential profits, then they will hire more workers. The income tax rate on the business has nothing to do with it. What is needed to make it all happen is consumer demand. The people who will do the buying in the economy are the ones who need the buying power to make it all happen. It is a consumer-driven economy. More income for the middle class, for the working poor and even for the non-workers will create demand. Consumer income and consumer confidence in the economy create jobs.

I mentioned consumer confidence. What about business confidence? Business confidence starts with consumer demand. If the masses in the population aren't buying, then there won't be any business confidence. Businesses prefer stable government policies for sure, but most business owners won't tell you that stable higher income tax rates will create just as much business confidence, in terms of creating jobs, as stable lower income tax rates. But that is the truth. Eliminating loopholes will create more stability than anything, because it levels the playing field. Businesses will quit scrambling around, paying expensive tax lawyers and accountants to look for loopholes if the loopholes no longer exist.

The rich benefit financially, and directly, from the infrastructure more than the poor do. The rich benefit from the spending patterns of the poor, through investments. The more money the poor have to spend, the more income the rich make off of domestic investments. Businesses (and investments) are successful only if the economy produces enough demand.

So, you don't want to raise taxes on "job creators"? Then quit demanding that the poor pay more taxes. Quit backing policies that have been destroying the middle class for the past 30 years. Prior to 1981, incomes for all classes rose together as the economy grew. The upper classes got more than the lower classes, but all gained at equivalent rates. Since then, the top 10% have received more than the rest. Even the gains of the top 10% have paled in comparisons to the gains of the top 1%. Those are economic facts that are readily available to anybody who cares to fact-check any of this. All of this is the result of changes in economic policies in Washington. These policies have created a situation in which income that would have been distributed throughout all income levels, based on policies that were in effect throughout the 1950s all the way through 1980, is now all going directly to the top. And this income is staying at the top. It is not trickling down. Wealth has been redistributed; but not from rich to poor like the political rhetoric says. Wealth never gets redistributed from rich to poor in the United States today. It always gets redistributed from poor and middle class to rich. The wealthiest have always received the most income, as a group. But the redistribution has occurred because of policy changes that have allowed them to keep all of the income gains, including the income that used to go to the middle-class. The American Dream of upward mobility is available to fewer and fewer people.

How does this affect the overall economy? What I am talking about has nothing to do with a sense of "fairness" or "equality" or anything like that. I am talking about the overall economy. Here is how the economy works in a nutshell:

The economy is comprised of people who buy, and people who sell. When enough goods and services get bought and sold, then the economy thrives. When enough goods and services don't get bought and sold, then the economy goes into a recession. The basic economy is the buyer and seller relationship. When things are going well, then this relationship is going well. When things are not going well, then this relationship is not going well. It's as simple as that. There are other things that influence the economy in very big ways. These are all familiar actors in the economy: the government, the banks, the import/export market, the Federal Reserve, even the weather. These are all things that influence the economy for better or worse. But their influence, good or bad, only matters to the extent that they affect the buyer and seller relationship. We have had 30-some years of policies that designed to benefit only one side of this relationship, and the economy has gotten out of whack. Top income tax rates, for individuals and for corporations, have been much lower since 1980 than they were in the decades before 1980, when the economy and the middle class were growing and stronger than they are now. These past 30-some years have also been years of deregulation for corporations, in the name of economic growth that has not materialized.

You can't have a full recovery from a deep recession without restoring the balance between buyer and seller. Free market economics, capitalism, is based on free transactions in which both sides to every transaction are equal. Continuously giving more to one side at the expense of the other side does not promote free markets, it destroys them. I don't care what the rhetoric says. Free markets need both sides of all transactions to have economic power.

But, you may say, the rich spend their money just like the poor and middle class do. Wrong! If they did, they would all be paying the maximum tax rate on all of their income. But they don't even come close. Instead of spending their money on consumer goods that the economy produces, creating demand and jobs, the rich put much of it in tax shelters that mostly do not create jobs. The poor and middle-class, on the other hand, spend most of their incomes on goods and services that the economy produces. In economics terms, this is called the marginal propensity to consume. The poor have a very high one, and the rich have a very low one.

Which brings up another hot issue that is driven by rhetoric: why raise taxes on the rich when they already pay most of the taxes? Well, they pay most of the income taxes, but not most of the other taxes. The other taxes are mostly regressive. The income tax used to be very progressive to balance this out. History shows that rhetoric stating that our current problems are caused by "oppressive" income taxes on rich individuals and corporations is untrue. Between 1950 and 1980, the top marginal income tax rates for individuals varied from time to time, ranging between 70% and 92%; at the same time, the top marginal income tax rates for corporations ranged between 42% and 52.8%. Compare that to the same rates between 1982 and 2013: 28% to 50% for individuals and 34% to 46% for corporations. The economy and the middle class grew more during the decades with the higher income tax rates; real wages for workers were higher.

But policies of the past 30 years have taken away much of the balance. The rich end up paying more income taxes because the policies have given them a much larger share of the income, and put more people under the taxable limit for income. Higher taxes on the rich didn't create a situation where the rich pay more income taxes - lower taxes on the rich did. The share of total taxes paid by the rich has gone up due to the rich having a much higher share of the total income, but the share of their income that is taken away in taxes has gone way down, to historically low levels. Policies in Washington have created this situation. Taking away money from those who earn it in order to give it to those who don't earn it? That has already been done. The working class has had their incomes confiscated and given to the very rich. The concept of "they earn it, so let them keep it" makes little sense when changes in policy have determined who receives it. Why should that concept apply after the policy changes but not before the policy changes?

Whether the wealthy are actually "earning" this redistribution or not, it is going to happen. The fact that it happens is not proof that it is somehow "earned"; the system says it is going to happen anyway. Arguing that it is their money that they have "earned" is a classic circular argument ["They receive it because they earn it". "How do you know that they earn it?" "I know because they receive it"].

The wages paid to workers used to go up when their productivity went up. The economy thrived when that happened. But for the past 30 years, workers' wages have not gone up while the workers' productivity has skyrocketed. This is not some liberal rhetoric. This is not some liberal theory. This is economic fact.

The result of the policies of the past 30 years is that the wealth gap and income gap between the very rich and everybody else are the highest that they have been since just before the Great Depression. We are seeing signs that this is no mere coincidence.

When financial investments earn income for investors, but do not create jobs, they create bubbles instead. These bubbles will eventually burst; guess who pays when they do? Oh, and one more "investment" that contributes to the problem: Political donations to support politicians who promise to maintain this system.

Use this Approach to Fix the Economy

Philosophy alone will not fix real-world problems in the economy. Advocating the use of the same policy for every type of perceived problem, based on a specific political philosophy, is more likely to compound existing problems or create new problems than it is to fix any real problems. Philosophy alone will not work. What is needed is a rational, consistent approach to problem identification and solving; not a consistent answer that covers every problem, but a consistent approach that will identify which answer will work for each specific situation.

I suggest that the following problem-solving approach should be used to fix an ailing economy:

(1) Recognize that the economy works only as well as a healthy business/consumer relationship exists;

(2) Look for bottlenecks in the business/consumer relationship;

(3) Use that information to figure out which areas to look into for the sources of the problems;

(4) After, never before, the sources of the problem have been identified using this approach, make suggested corrections that will eliminate the causes of the problems.

Futility is trying to "fix" what ails the economy by twisting reality to fit some preconceived philosophical or political position, and then applying a "fix" that is consistent with that philosophy. This approach won't fix anything because it works backwards: it applies the "fix" first, and then spins real world conditions in order to identify the problems that match the fix. This approach starts with philosophy, and has "reality" being derived from a spin on the philosophy.

The only way to assure that the end result is likely to be a workable solution is to start with the reality. The reality must come first, not the philosophy. Find out where the economy has gone wrong based solely on where the bottlenecks are; take a closer look at those bottlenecks and their causes. Focus on those causes - there is really no need at this point to focus on measurements such as GDP, unemployment, or inflation. Measurements can be misleading, and will take care of themselves if the focus is on fixing the causes of the problems. Obsessing over specific measurements will not help to identify and solve real problems. In the big picture, you don't need measurements to know if economic growth is slow, if too many people are out of work, or if inflation is a problem. Statistics are too easy to spin. A focus on specific measurements is just as likely to be a philosophical spin on reality as it is a tool for identifying real problems. Only after the focus is placed properly on the causes of the problems can a policy that will work be decided. Perhaps after the specific causes of the problems are identified, philosophy may play a role in the proposed solutions; but only after identifying the sources of the problems - not before that point.

I should point out that I have not been able to identify any time or place in history in which the economy ran so smoothly that no problems could be identified. The real world has not provided perfection. Economic systems are created by humans, and no system has provided perfection. However, in the real world, regardless of the system, the business cycle is real. The economy goes through a series of ups and downs, experiencing times when it is running relatively smoothly, and times when widespread problems are obviously present. I point out this lack of perfection in order to make the case that this problem solving technique can be an ongoing process, in seemingly good times as well as bad times. Such an ongoing approach can provide economic stability, an alternative to frequent crisis-management mode for policy-makers, and a process that permanently lessens the problems associated with the extremes of the business cycle. In the absence of a rational, consistent approach to problem-solving, we instead have instability created by rigid adherence to competing philosophies by politicians motivated to make political points and collect campaign donations.

To illustrate this problem solving technique, let's start with the basics of how the economy works when things are going relatively smoothly:

In order for the economy to run smoothly, businesses must be willing and able to sell; consumers must be willing and able to buy. That's it. The economy works smoothly when this happens. This outcome of the business/consumer relationship is the underlying, but often unspoken, basis behind the different economic philosophies. The outcome of the business/consumer relationship is the only thing that matters when determining if the economy is working well or not. Advocates of various philosophies, however, have tended to set aside this business/consumer relationship in order to focus on other players in the system, and make one-size-fits-all judgments on these other players. The "other players" include governments; the labor market; the international market; the Federal Reserve; the banking system; and stock, bond, and commodity markets, among others. Judgments on these other players become the unifying factors of specific philosophies. Instead of a focus on the outcome of the business/consumer relationship, the focus is on the judgment of the other players in the system. Instead of policies that focus on the specific situation at hand, we get policies based on a one-size-fits-all philosophy, such as "government is always bad".

One-size-fits-all judgments do not fix real problems because they take the focus away from the actual situation at hand. These "other players" certainly have huge influences on the economy, in a number of ways and for a number of reasons. It is fashionable but not rational to assume that all real and potential problems are caused by one or more of these 'other players" based solely on philosophical judgments rather than the reality of each situation. In the above example, how do we know that "government is always bad"? We only know that because the judgment created by our philosophy tells us what to know. This judgment can and does create situations in which policies designed to fix problems actually compound the same problems. Instead of focusing on the philosophical judgments, a rational approach would be to focus on the business/consumer relationship.

When there are problems with how the economy is working, then something is wrong with this business/consumer relationship. Bottlenecks exist in the system. To solve the problems, the bottlenecks and their sources need to be identified, and then a proper policy can be applied to deal specifically with the existing problems. Instead of using preconceived judgments to automatically place blame, find the bottlenecks in the business/consumer relationship, and then deal with the bottlenecks. It may very well turn out that in any specific case, something about the government (or whatever "player" your one-size-fits-all judgment decides to blame) has created the bottleneck. But it won't be true just because your philosophical judgment says it is true.

Instead of using pre-conceived judgments, focus on the real economy and the business/consumer relationship. Keep the focus on these four questions:

Are businesses willing to sell? Are businesses able to sell? Are consumers willing to buy? Are consumers able to buy?

Those are the questions to ask before assigning any blame, focusing on any details, or proposing any solutions. The answers to those questions will tell you where to look for problems as well as solutions. A "no" answer to any of the above questions means that a bottleneck exists. When you determine that an answer to one of the questions is "no", take a closer look at the situation in order to identify what specifically caused the answer to be "no". After the bottlenecks are found, take a closer look at the causes of the bottlenecks. It could very well be that these "other players" have contributed to or solely caused the problems. It is important to look at these other players only after the bottleneck has been identified; otherwise, reality will be clouded by philosophical judgment with the result being a "solution" that does not match the problem. The only determining factor should be whether specific actions of these players hinder or help the business/consumer relationship. These "other players" do indeed affect the economy in big ways; the only thing that is important for solving problems in the economy is to determine, for specific situations, whether and how the influence of these players is a positive or negative influence on the business/consumer relationship.

I repeat for emphasis: These "other players" (government, etc.) are important and can be the source of problems, but only to the extent that they negatively affect the basic business/consumer relationship. In order to identify problems with the performance of the economy, we first need to find where the business/consumer relationship breaks down, and then look at these outside influences for potential sources of those problems.

This should be the approach: Look for bottlenecks in the business/consumer relationship by asking if consumers and businesses are willing and able to play their roles in the economy; and then use that information to figure out which areas to look for in order to determine the sources of the problems. Then, and only then, can you rationally make suggested corrections that will eliminate the causes of the problems.

For an example that is relevant and timely, try using this approach on the current state of the United States economy. It should be obvious that huge problems exist, so there should be nothing to gain by trying to discover IF there are problems; we already know that problems are present.

Using this approach to analyze the situation, ask these four questions: Are businesses willing to sell? Are businesses able to sell? Are consumers willing to buy? Are consumers able to buy? If the answer to any of these questions is yes, then there is no problem in that area; look somewhere else for problems. Don't try to fix a problem that doesn't exist. On the other hand, if the answer is no, then you have identified that a bottleneck exists in that area. A problem for the economy has been traced to that area. At this point, the focus should be in that area in order to determine which outside influences have contributed to the problem.

So what are the answers to these four questions as they apply to the current United States economy?

Are businesses willing to sell?

This is a little bit complicated, with evidence that seems to conflict. The answer seems to vary based on sizes and types of businesses. Businesses range from small, local mom and pop stores to giant multi-national corporations. Businesses exist for manufacturing, retail, service, and other industries. The answer to the question seems to depend, at least in part, on the specific size and type of business. For the most part, businesses choose to invest wherever profit potential is highest. It appears that for many types of businesses, the option of downsizing in order to cut costs is a current strategy for increasing short term profits. Perhaps this is not a sustainable strategy; perhaps, as many corporate executives claim, they cannot find enough workers with the correct skills. Many larger businesses, especially corporations, are finding more profit potential in foreign markets. Cost is a consideration, especially cost savings associated with production in third-world economies; tax benefits of offshore profits are a consideration; but the consumer base is also a consideration. With domestic incomes down, corporations are looking elsewhere for new sales. There is a potential bottleneck here, and some of it appears to be related to consumer demand. Since we cannot get a definite "yes" answer to this question, let's mark it as an area where a potential bottleneck exists. This is one area where we should look for specific bottlenecks and their sources. The answer appears to be complicated; perhaps worthy of public debate.

Are businesses able to sell?

If you look at the "big picture", you will find that most large, multi-national corporations are more than able to sell. Profits have soared even as the world has been trying to recover from a recession. Many corporations are sitting on record cash levels. The cost of borrowing (interest rates) is at an all-time low. Funds for investing in new production are readily available. As measured by stock prices, corporations in general are thriving. Profits, fund availability, and stock prices all indicate that corporations are definitely able to sell. For our approach to problem solving, it doesn't make sense to look for a solution that is designed to give corporations the ability to sell. That would be a solution where no problem exists; look elsewhere for problems to fix. Unfortunately, because policy-makers rely on philosophical judgments instead of a rational approach to problem solving, this is the "solution" that we end up with more often than not. The solution doesn't match the problem. It is little wonder that such policies have not resulted in any improvements in the business/consumer relationship, or the overall performance of the economy.

The answer to the question "are businesses able to sell?" is a resounding "yes". No bottleneck exists here, so we need to look elsewhere for potential problems. But wait – the reasons given for the "yes" answer all relate to large corporations. What about small businesses? Are they able to sell?

The answer for small businesses is not the same as the answer for large corporations. Funds are not necessarily available. After the Great Recession of 2007-2009, credit tightened up considerably. The credit situation has eased somewhat, so at the present time this situation is a bit fluid. But the availability of funds is still an overall problem for small businesses. Many small businesses continue to fail due to competition from large corporations. Deregulation of large corporations and a government policy of not using antitrust laws to protect small businesses contribute to the problem. At the same time, regulations and taxes for small businesses might be taking away from the ability of these businesses to sell. We definitely have a bottleneck here, and we have a good start on identifying the sources. A rational policy for fixing the problem would focus on the sources, as identified by this process.

Before we move on to the rest of the questions, we should note that the answers to the questions about businesses, as well as the sources of the problems that the process identifies, can be and often are different depending on whether the businesses are small businesses or large corporations. Now that we have noted this difference, let's move on to the rest of the questions.

Are consumers willing to buy?

We cannot give a resounding "yes" answer to this question. Therefore, this is an area where potential bottlenecks exist. We need to take a closer look.

We have an economy in which we have a high number of people who are unemployed; a high number of people who have given up and quit looking for work; a high number of people who are forced to work part time, perhaps in jobs unrelated to their skills, when they would prefer to work full time; real incomes of many workers are decreasing; and a high number of people whose wealth and income are decreasing due to a combination of a down economy and an aging population. Being unemployed, with lower income, doesn't give a "no" answer to the question of willingness to buy, at least not directly. But indirectly it does, because for many people in this economy, the prospects of individual financial situations turning worse results in many people being afraid to spend as much as they would otherwise. It makes people less willing to add to future credit payment obligations. When this situation applies to a lot of people at the same time, it creates a "no" answer to the question of whether consumers on the aggregate are willing to buy in quantities necessary for sustaining a well-functioning economy. There is definitely a bottleneck in this area, and potentially several different sources for this bottleneck. In addition to the above reasons for a "no" answer to this question, there is a somewhat mysterious phenomenon going on with workers. For some reason, even as the population is aging, more young workers are choosing not to participate in the labor market at all. They are not employed, and they don't want to look for work. This phenomenon has been identified by the same polls that are used to determine the unemployment rate. Does this also represent a bottleneck in the economy? In order to properly answer this question, we need to look into this situation more closely and follow a rational approach to problem solving instead of passing philosophical judgments.

Are consumers able to buy?

In the aggregate, in quantities necessary for sustaining a well-functioning economy, the answer to this question is a resounding "no". This is definitely bottleneck territory. High unemployment, a smaller labor force participation rate, changing demographics, smaller real incomes for those who are working, and a rapidly-shrinking middle class all contribute to a very real problem with low consumer demand. Without a significant amount of consumer demand, there can be no workable business/consumer relationship. We have already identified many causes of this bottleneck. We need to look at the sources of those causes, in order to rationally identify potential solutions.

So far, we have looked at all of the questions and identified potential areas where bottlenecks might exist. At this point, we can eliminate everything else as potential problems. If a "solution" doesn't directly address an identified bottleneck, it is not a rational solution. Such a solution will solve nothing, and it potentially can make existing problems worse or create new problems.

We know which questions have potential "no" answers. From this point forward, all of the focus should be in these areas. We have identified many of the problems that contribute to the "no" answers. What is left is to use this information to look into each situation in more detail, and come up potential policies which will provide real solutions to real problems. We can now look at activities involving the "other players" in the economy to see where the bottlenecks are coming from. We don't need any one-size-fits-all judgment of these "other players"; we have moved beyond that. We are focusing on real problems, not philosophy. Are any of these "other players" contributing to the problem? If so, then how? Are any of these "other players" actually helping to alleviate problems? Do they have the potential to help "fix" the known problems? The problem solving process is working; the details need to be worked out. Once the real sources of the problems are identified, it is possible for philosophy to play a role in proposals – but not before the sources of the problems have been identified.

But look at what happens when the philosophy comes first, instead of a rational process. In our exercise, we have identified many potential problems. Most of them deal with issues that decrease consumer demand. Lack of consumer demand is clearly the biggest problem, and this problem potentially has several different sources. Some of the potential problems deal with the inability of small businesses to compete with large corporations. None of the potential problems deal with the ability of large corporations to be able to sell. Yet what kinds of policies do we get from politicians who are dealing with these real problems? Instead of using a rational approach to problem-solving, they have relied on a philosophy-first process. As a result, we get policies that are designed to "fix" the one thing that we can identify as not being the problem: the ability of large corporations to sell. Many of these policies make it harder for small businesses to compete; to a very large extent, many of these policies decrease the ability and willingness of consumers to buy. The "solution" makes real problems worse, and "fixes" a non-existent problem; it is not a rational approach, and the result is a set of policies that are not helping to fix real problems.

I want to make one final comment. In this exercise, we used the current United States economy as an example for this approach. We have noted that the U.S. economy currently has many obvious problems, and indeed we did come up with many "no" answers, and each of these "no" answers in turn has several potential sources for real problems. As a result, some of the answers in the initial stage that has been presented here are fairly complicated. This result should be expected for an economy that obviously is not running smoothly. During better economic times, we would expect to have "yes" and "no" answers that are more clearly-defined, fewer "no" answers, and fewer potential sources associated with each one.

Here Is a Novel Approach to Education Reform

Here is a novel approach to education reform.

Instead of taking corporate money in exchange for letting corporations dictate education policy based on their bottom line concerns, why not try this:

Make sure these corporations are paying their fair share of taxes at both the federal and state levels. Then, use a portion of that money to fund education.

This will improve education:

Education policy can be based on the actual goals of the education system instead of the profit motive of corporations.

Professional educators, not profit-hungry managers, will determine more of the policy. This will create an incentive for politicians to listen to the education professionals more, to the corporate CEOs less.

With tight budgets, especially at the state level where education consumes a large percentage of the budgets, public schools will be more adequately funded.

With educators having a larger say in policy, those who love to teach, and are motivated by their accomplishments as teachers, will stay in the profession. The teaching profession will be able to attract more of the best into the profession to begin with.

With educators having a larger say in policy, funds can be directed to where they are needed most to achieve the overall goals of the education system, instead of simply being directed to where they can improve the bottom lines of selected corporations.

Perhaps students will be able to find what they are good at, and what they are interested in, instead of having all funding at all grade levels being funneled into "core" subjects. The arts won't have to suffer, social sciences won't have to suffer, and the "core" subjects at higher grade levels will attract those who are best in those subjects.

Perhaps, just perhaps, teachers will be compensated according to the requirements that they have to meet in order to enter the profession. Perhaps teachers will get respect for their abilities, their sacrifices, and the on the job experience, instead of being blamed for society's problems. Perhaps even the teachers' burden of paying for school supplies out of their own pockets can be alleviated.

As a bonus, this will also improve the economy:

Money that is now being used to fatten corporate profits, pay millions in executive salaries, invest in overseas jobs, and for political contributions to protect all of this will be redirected towards something that will actually create American jobs. More students will be taught to think creatively for a changing global economy, instead of a narrower focus of "bubbling for corporate shareholders". More entrepreneurship-thinking, less CEO-thinking, is how future jobs will be created.

Corporations will have more incentive to actually create jobs. If their marginal tax rates are increased, and everybody knows that they don't like to pay taxes, then they will have more of an incentive to take the tax write-off that comes with investing in human capital. They have enough money now to invest in jobs, but are not doing so. Increasing their tax rates on the profits that are not invested in jobs will help to give them the incentive that they need.

States can quit engaging in a race to the bottom. Currently, states are using tax incentives to lure businesses away from other states. This is a zero-sum game that creates no wealth and no jobs for the overall economy. Since no wealth and no jobs are created, the net result of these tax incentives is lower tax revenues for all states combined. This money could instead be available for education funding.

With a more progressive tax code, the middle class can start growing again. A strong middle class is necessary for the long term health of the economy, for economic growth, for improving the standard of living. The middle class provides the necessary ingredients to make the economy function properly: consumer demand, labor, savings, and investment. The middle class is also necessary to maintain hopes of achieving the American dream of upward mobility. In the long run, business confidence begins with a healthy middle class.

With tight state and federal budgets, the burden for funding public schools often falls on property owners in the form of property taxes, and on local taxpayers in the form of education bonds and local-option sales taxes. Putting more tax revenue from corporations into the federal and state budgets will alleviate this burden on American citizens at the local level.

Since the burden of funding currently falls more at the local level, and policy currently is dictated at the federal level, the American goals of universal education and equal opportunity are being lost. With current policy as well as current reform efforts, we are moving away from, not towards, these goals. Giving education professionals more say in policy, and taking more of the burden of education funding away from local citizens, will put policy more in line with these goals.

Obviously, nothing like this is possible in today's political climate. To many people, this will look like nothing more than wishful thinking. It will take actions of many, not the words of one, to change the climate. Politicians and American voters would have to be aware, to understand the problems with the current realities, as well as the realities of what is possible.

This requires some fundamental changes in the public's thinking process. No one person or small group of persons can change that many minds in a short period of time. But the more the word gets out, the shorter and less painful the process of true reform needs to be. There are visible signs that the momentum is shifting, that public opinion is slowly turning around. We are seeing a backlash against "reform" in a number of jurisdictions.

You Heard it Here First: The US Government Does Not Run a Budget Deficit, Ever.

It's true. When the bills come due, the bills get paid. The federal government never defaults on its obligations. The only thing that can prevent a balanced budget would be if Congress refused to increase the debt limit.

You might be screaming right now. "This is absurd! This is idiotic! Of course the government doesn't balance its budget every year. The bills get paid because the government increases its debt, not because the government takes in enough revenue. That is not balancing the budget!"

Okay, you have a point. These are not balanced budgets if revenue isn't enough to cover the expenditures. I admit it, my earlier statement is false. The historical fact is that the U.S. government rarely balances its budget.

By the same token, and using the same definition, households and businesses don't always balance the budget either. I am using an absurd statement about the government balancing its budget in order to make a different point about equally absurd political rhetoric used to equate government spending with household and business spending.

When a household puts anything on credit that doesn't get paid off right away, it is running a deficit. When people take out mortgages to be paid off over a long period of time; when they take on car payments, credit card payments, student loans, bank loans, and any other obligation where the entire obligation is not paid off in the same year, then they are running a deficit. The same way the government runs a deficit.

Businesses routinely use credit. Not just to cover start-up costs, major expansions, and unexpected catastrophes, but for a host of other reasons. Large businesses hire expensive tax attorneys and accountants to tell them when and how to leverage, when increasing debt is in their best interest. Using the same definition that you use for government, businesses don't always balance their budgets either.

The federal government covers its budget shortfall by offering treasury securities for sale to the public. The public buys these up because they are considered the safest investments in the entire world. Even when the ratings agencies decided to downgrade these securities, the prices went up because the public trusts these investments and the ratings don't matter. What becomes debt for the government is an investment for investors, and a very popular one.

The point I am trying to make is this: Statements such as

"Government deficits are wrong because we the people always have to live within our budgets; the government should too"

and

"Government deficits are wrong because businesses have to pay their bills and the government should too"

are simply invalid arguments. Those are meaningless words, but people make those kinds of statements all the time.

Those kinds of statements can only be true if you take the same definition of deficits that I used for the government when I made the claim that the government never runs a deficit, and apply it to households and businesses; while at the same time, use a different definition for the same term and apply it to the government. Applying a different definition for deficits to the government than you do to households and businesses, and then making arguments as if they are the same things, is non sequitur. It simply is not valid. The statement that I made above, that the government always balances its budget, is false. I only made that statement in order to point out the equally absurd argument that the government should be forced to balance its budget every year because households and businesses have to.

I could stop right here. I have made my point. But if I leave it at this, I can just see a lot of people saying something like "he just said that deficits are good". No, I did not say that. Don't read into this something that is not here and argue against what you are reading into it. Doing so would be a straw man argument; also invalid.

I also did not say that the government is the same as a household or a business. I said that the definition of a deficit should be consistently applied when comparing governments, households, and businesses. But I did not say that these entities are the same. There are important differences when it comes to the wisdom of deficit spending. Important similarities also exist.

First, the similarities: Think in terms of opportunity cost. Debt, whether undertaken by individuals, households, businesses, or governments, is undertaken for the purpose of gaining something. It is a trade-off. If the benefits of any specific instance of deficit spending outweigh the costs, relative to other options, then adding to debt would be a wise choice. If the costs outweigh the benefits, then doing so would not be wise. If a different option creates a better net benefit, then deficit spending is not wise. The true cost of any decision is the opportunity cost. Deficit spending is an investment in the future, and this investment can be wise or unwise. For many people, the debt associated with a mortgage is a wise trade-off for home ownership. Many other people choose never to go into debt. They choose to pay for everything out of money that they have already received. The trade-off for these people is a limited ability to make large-ticket purchases as well as a limited ability to increase their standard of living. Unless somebody gives them a large sum of money somewhere, most people cannot increase their standard of living very much without taking on some debt somewhere along the line. Debt can be looked on as an investment in the future, so deciding to forgo debt means forgoing that particular investment. The same thing can be said for government spending. The wisdom of each choice is not clear until all of the costs and benefits have been factored in.

But there are important differences. One obvious difference is that the federal government gets to print its own money. Also, the government gets to make the rules. These facts can make adding to debt seem less painful in the short run. It means that the government could have incentives to add to debt without a full cost/benefit analysis. But it does not mean that government debt is always bad, and that the cost of debt to taxpayers is always higher than the benefits. It does mean that we as taxpayers need to be vigilant. We need to be fully aware of all potential costs and benefits. For example, there are safeguards in place that are designed to give the government an incentive to make these decisions based on net benefit; the big-picture benefits to shoot for are even defined for the government. Do you know what these safeguards are, which ways they work, and which ways they fail? Do you know the historical record of the economic outcomes of various spending decisions?

I'll mention one other important difference. Households consume goods and services. Businesses produce goods and services. The U.S. government does neither. Spending means different things for these three types of entities. Because of this, the costs and benefits are going to be different.

"Wait", you may say. Government spending IS consumption. No, it isn't, not when you are doing a cost/benefit analysis based on opportunity costs. When the government spends, it is acting as sort of a middleman for the private sector. Everything that the government does affects both consumption and production in the private sector. These effects can be huge. They can be negative effects. But they also can be positive effects. Government services provide the means for private industry and the economy to function.

All government actions affect the economy. These actions can have positive effects, and they can have negative effects. Each situation is different. It is up to citizens to monitor their government and hold it responsible. But this requires a cost/benefit analysis of individual situations. It doesn't serve any useful purpose to make a simplistic statement such as "the government is always the problem" or "the private sector can do everything that the government can do, only better". Those kinds of statements might have strong political appeal and emotional appeal, but they are extremely easy to prove false. Attempts to justify them usually involve arguments of sweeping generalization as well as ad nauseam, both logical fallacies. Sweeping generalization means that an obvious conclusion reached from some specific situation is used as evidence that a specific conclusion will "always" result in every other situation. Ad nauseam means that the same line, the same truism, is repeated so often that many people hearing them come to the conclusion that they must be true, so these people ignore the real evidence to the contrary.

Government spending can and does have positive aspects, but also negative aspects. It makes sense to look at these aspects for specific situations. It does not make sense to avoid looking at the real costs and benefits by making fallacious sweeping generalizations. Part of the cost/benefit analysis for government spending involves the decision to pay for expenditures with current tax revenue (and the decision on how and from whom to raise this revenue) or to pay for expenditures with additional debt. Each one of these options has its own advantages and disadvantages; and just as in the private sector, a combination of current revenue and new debt can be the best answer.

What about the idea of lowering total government spending just for its own sake? Apply the same kind of cost/benefit analysis. Do you know the actual results, the costs and benefits, from applying opposing policies on this in different situations? There is a very large historical record on this; do you know what it is? Do you know the difference between the statements of simplicity, the rhetoric, and the actual record? There is no need to cite old theories based on controlled circumstances that do not exist in the real world; there is an actual real world record. And do you know the difference between the rhetoric and the actual wording of the Constitution, for cases where the Constitution is brought up in the arguments?

As a convenience, I have included the full text of the U.S. Constitution in the appendix to this book. For more details on topics covered in this essay, see the following pages from the Economics Online Tutor website:

Deficits and the National Debt

The Effectiveness of Discretionary Fiscal Policy

U.S. Economics History: Performance and Politics in One Simplified Table

The Real World Is Like a Game of Monopoly with No Winners

Okay, Monopoly may be only a game. One person ends up with everything; everybody else loses everything. The one with everything wins bragging rights, and anything else the players might have agreed to. But what are the real life implications?

The game of Monopoly is all about economic success and failure. But think about what happens after the winner is declared. There is no "happily ever after". What exactly does the winner get? Remember, the game is about economic success and failure. With that in mind, what does the winner get?

The winner owns all the real estate. During the game, as this real estate is being accumulated, the real estate is used to extract wealth from the other players in the game; in the real world, "other players in the game" would translate to "everybody else in the economy". As the eventual game winner accumulates more and more real estate, the "other players in the game" have less and less to contribute to the game. When the game is over, they have nothing to contribute. What good is this real estate to somebody who owns it all? How can it be of any financial value when nobody can afford to pay rent? The real estate will end up sitting idle, generating no wealth for winners or losers. You wind up with empty buildings while "everybody else in the economy" is hungry and homeless.

The winner owns all of the money. As the game progresses, and the eventual winner keeps accumulating more and more of the money, there is less and less money left to get. The economy slows down, eventually coming to a complete halt. What good does it do to have all of the money? Money has no value if nobody else has anything worth buying. Money becomes, well, Monopoly money in the figurative sense. The image of a medieval king doing nothing except counting all his money comes to mind.

So what can the "winner" do? What good is it to own all the wealth? Is it really wealth if it provides no tangible benefits? One option would be for the "winner", who is now a monopolist, to hire some of those "everybody else in the economy", who got wiped out in the game, to produce something that they would buy. The monopolist will have no desire to give up wealth. The workers will get paid just enough to ensure that production takes place, nothing more. The incentive for the monopolist is to accumulate wealth. This won't be accomplished if the workers are paid according to what they produce; they will need to be paid as little as possible, to live off the "crumbs", so to speak. A good PR campaign will keep them happy. The monopolist just needs to convince the people that without the "generosity" of the monopolist, the people would have no jobs at all. It doesn't matter that before the monopolist "won" the game, these people had good-paying jobs. The monopolist can become somewhat of a hero in the minds of the people with a good PR campaign; he is now the benevolent "job creator". The people won't realize that without the monopolist taking all the wealth to begin with, there wouldn't have been a job void in the first place; or a society living off the crumbs of the wealthy.

This is one option for the monopolist, but this option is a losing battle from the beginning. No rational monopolist would consider using this strategy alone. The monopolist expects to make more than the workers. Where is this profit going to come from if the people only get their money from the monopolist? An additional strategy is needed. The monopolist would have to find customers with money to spend; customers in addition to the "other players in the game". Who are these customers? They have to be people who are not part of "everybody else in the economy". They would have to be people who weren't in the game at all. The overall economy will have to be redefined to include foreigners who can become customers. The domestic economy would have to succeed on the strength of exports. This might work in the short run. But what would happen in the long run?

If the foreign markets are strong enough to provide profits for the monopolist, then even more profits can be achieved by moving production to where the customers are; costs can be lowered in the process, even more so if the customers exist in a country with a third-world-but-growing economy. Who needs domestic sales, when the only money that domestic customers have comes from the "crumbs" of the monopolist? Here is where another PR campaign can come in handy for the monopolist. The domestic workers face the real threat of having their jobs shipped overseas. A good PR campaign will convince them that the jobs are leaving because of "high" domestic labor costs. The people now will be willing to work for even less than the "crumbs" that they were making before. The people who are so grateful to the "job creators" will be convinced that they are overpaid, even while working for less than a living wage!

This outcome from the game of Monopoly is being played out in the real world, right here in the richest part of the world. The above scenario is the natural outcome of unregulated, "free" markets in which policies always favor the "job creator". Giving the "sellers" free reign does not produce the theoretical outcomes of economic efficiency caused by increased competition. The opposite occurs. Competition is drastically decreased, continuously. The natural outcome would be the above scenario, with only one "seller" in the entire economy.

We haven't reached that extreme outcome yet. We have yet to get to the point where the economy consists of only one seller, with a near-total reliance on foreign sales and almost "free" labor domestically. But we are headed in that direction, and very quickly. Competition is decreasing rapidly, as fewer companies control larger market shares; as competition decreases, the surviving corporations are branching out into more and more markets; more and more workers are being paid less than a livable wage, even as productivity and profits skyrocket; many of these workers have been convinced that the system is good for them because of the benevolence of "job creators", even though more jobs, and a living wage, would be available without so much economic power going to fewer corporations; masses of people have less money to spend, so the economy can produce fewer jobs and smaller economic growth; in the name of "free markets", society has to deal with a growing number of working people who cannot subsist on market wages.

The only solution is to return to a system in which labor is actually paid according to productivity. Free reign for corporations in an unregulated economy will not provide that. An insistence on a living wage, taxing offshore profits, and eliminating the concept of "too big to fail" will. But in order to get there, we have to deal with the fact that millions of people have bought into the PR campaigns designed to convince them that they will somehow lose their personal freedoms if they are forced to accept a living wage.

What about "taking money away from those who earn it"? The truth is, as long as there is a divergence between labor productivity and wages, this redistribution is already occurring. In modern-day America, wealth never gets redistributed from the wealthy to the poor. Wealth always moves from the poor to the wealthy, and the middle class quickly disappears in the process. The historical data overwhelmingly support this truth. The divergence between productivity and wages has been

going on since the beginning of the 1980s, and corresponds to
fundamental changes in economic policy.

What is a Chained-CPI Index? Why is it controversial?

First, some background concerning inflation and price indexes:

Prices and wages do not always move together. They do not all move at the same rate, at the same time, or even always in the same direction. This means that during any specific time frame, inflation will affect different people in varying degrees. Price indexes have been developed as an attempt to measure the average effect of inflation on different groups of people. Changes in consumer prices are measured using an index called the Consumer Price Index, or CPI.

Given that the economy is large and complex, these measurements are estimates; they are attempts at measuring average, not actual, effects on individuals within a group. The CPI is a calculation by the Bureau of Labor Statistics, a calculation which measures price changes in what is considered to be a "typical" bundle of goods purchased by a "typical" household in a given period of time.

The CPI is a measurement of the loss of purchasing power due to inflation for a specific dollar amount of income for consumers. The loss of purchasing power for people on a "fixed" income can be offset by tying the incomes of these people to the CPI. That is the purpose; that is the theory behind cost of living increases (COLAs) for people who rely on Social Security benefits for their living expenses.

The CPI is a flawed measurement, for a number of reasons:

1. As mentioned above, it is only an estimate of an average.

2. The CPI is not adjusted for different spending patterns of different individuals, and especially for differences in spending

among different demographic groups. There is no such thing as a "typical" household that spends income according to a predetermined "typical" bundle of goods. Of specific interest here, the demographic groups that comprise those who rely on Social Security benefits tend to have spending patterns that are far different from other demographic groups that are used in the CPI calculations. Many people believe that senior citizens tend to lose purchasing power over time due to a downward bias in the CPI calculations for this demographic group.

3. Using one measurement, whether it is the CPI or some other measurement, can never be accurate because of the difference between something called "core inflation" and something called "headline inflation". Certain items that tend to make up a large percentage of many people's spending patterns, such as food and energy, tend to have volatile price changes relative to other price changes. Over longer periods of time, these "headline" items tend to have price changes that are similar to other "core" items; but in the short run, price changes for the headline items are much more volatile. When gasoline prices go up quickly, or even when meat prices go up, headline inflation is much higher than core inflation. But at other times, headline inflation is much lower than core inflation, to the extent that overall headline inflation can be negative (deflation) while core inflation is positive. The differences between the "headline" and "core" measurements of inflation in any given time period have different implications depending on the context of what the measurements are being used for. For example, monetary policy based on headline inflation measurements would be very volatile and could further destabilize the economy. For this reason, the CPI only measures core inflation. People who rely on Social Security benefits tend to spend a relatively large percentage of income on headline items, leading to charges that the formula used to calculate COLAs for people on Social Security lead to a decrease in purchasing power for seniors; that inflation is

understated for these people, especially during times of rising gasoline prices.

4. Over time, product quality tends to change due to new technology and the introduction of new features on existing products. Many things become "new and improved" and today's products may be vastly different from their counterparts from yesteryear. The CPI index does not take into consideration that these added features mean that consumers may get more out of each product. The CPI does not measure how much of a price change is due to different features, and how much is due to a decrease in purchasing power. It treats all price increases as inflation and ignores the improvements. This works the other way, also. Some products are manufactured to be inferior to yesterday's versions. But overall, most economists consider the CPI to overstate inflation because it ignores technological improvements.

5. Another form of upward bias is known as the substitution effect. The CPI measurement over time is based on prices in a constant "typical bundle" of goods. However, when some prices tend to increase over time much more than other prices, people in the aggregate will spend less of their incomes on the products with the highest price increases, and spend more of their incomes on products with price decreases or at least lower price increases. Since the CPI uses only a constant bundle, regardless of the differences in individual price changes, it will overstate inflation by the magnitude of the substitution effect. Differences of opinion exist regarding the size of the substitution effect.

What is the Chained-CPI?

The Chained-CPI has been developed as an attempt to remove the upward bias due to the substitution effect as described in #5 above. Basically, it uses a "chained" bundle instead of a "fixed" bundle of goods in order to measure inflation. Up until now, a Chained-CPI has not been used as part of government policy. However, it is currently on the table in the budget negotiations; thus the current increase in public interest.

What are the controversies?

Just as the CPI is flawed because it uses estimates of what is "typical", the Chained-CPI takes these estimates to another level, making their accuracy even more "iffy". One reason why the Chained-CPI has not been adopted before now is the lack of confidence in its accuracy.

Although it has not been used in policy before now, the Chained-CPI has been tracked for some time. It clearly does provide a lower measure of inflation than the standard CPI currently in use. This lower inflation measure is important, because the Chained-CPI is being considered for calculating COLA's for Social Security benefits. A switch would clearly lead to lower future benefits for Social Security recipients. The argument in favor of switching to a Chained-CPI includes the upward bias of the substitution effect, as explained in #5 above. The argument is that adjustments for inflation are too high because the CPI overstates inflation. The counter-argument is that the people who are being targeted (Social Security recipients) already are facing decreasing purchasing power due to the points made in #2 and #3 above. According to this argument, the downward bias of the CPI, especially for the targeted senior citizens, far outweighs the upward bias due to a substitution effect that is not demographic-specific. Social Security benefits are already low for these reasons, and a switch to a Chained-CPI would make them even lower. Lower purchasing power and lower standards of living for our senior citizens would result. People who have paid into the system for decades would lose benefits that they have paid for.

One more area of controversy: The debate over the Chained-CPI is included in the debate over the federal budget, even though Social Security is not part of the general budget; Social Security is a separate fund with separate funding. Combining a debate over Social Security with a debate over the general budget confuses the issue, creating potential for misinformation in the public and in the media. A decrease in benefits has been tied to the debate over the future solvency of the Social Security system, and the urgency and wisdom of "doing something about it" now. But in its current form, that is not the issue being debated. The health of the Social Security system is an issue that involves much more than what is being discussed today. Instead of debating that issue and all of its specific complexities, a decrease in future Social Security benefits has been inserted into a largely unrelated budget debate.

How Investment in Infrastructure Helps Economic Recovery

Suppose you run a construction company. What is it about your company's business activities that contribute to the overall economy?

The specific kinds of construction projects affect the future economy in specific ways, whether they involve houses, apartment buildings, commercial buildings, schools, roads, or something else. But a construction company is merely a tool for these contributions. Somebody else decides what will be built and for what purpose, and shares in the risks and rewards associated with the final "product" that gets built. What is it about construction activities that in and of themselves contributes to the economy?

Construction creates income. The economy (GDP) can be measured by counting expenditures, or by counting income. This is because one person's expenditure is somebody else's income. For a construction project, whoever is "buying" pays the construction company. This creates income for the construction company, its employees, and its suppliers. The suppliers themselves benefit from an increase in demand, and have employees and suppliers to pay as well. The income received by the various parties becomes available in the economy. Consumers have more money to spend throughout the economy on goods and services that seemingly are unrelated to the construction business. Various businesses receive more demand, and more income, and the prospect of more profits becomes an incentive for business investment. The economy grows and jobs are created throughout the economy. This is called the multiplier effect.

One construction project can affect the economy in this manner to some extent. But the degree of economic growth and job creation can be multiplied several times over whenever many projects by many different construction companies occur at the same time. A boon in construction is a sign of a growing economy.

Now, back up to what I said above. This multiplier effect starts when "whoever is buying pays the construction company for the job". That is what starts the ball rolling, so to speak. But the effects on the economy do not depend on the identity of the "buyer". The same thing is going to happen whether the buyer is a private individual, company, or the government. In the United States, as well as many other countries, the government is not in the construction business. The government makes construction decisions, mostly for infrastructure building and repair, but the government contracts the work out to private companies. There is no difference between a private decision to build and a public decision to build in terms of the multiplier effect. Whether it is the government or private industry that decides to build, the chain of events that is the multiplier effect is going to be the same. Demand created by government spending in this case is the same as demand created in the marketplace. The effects on the overall economy - economic growth and job creation - are going to be the same.

The only difference between private and public construction decisions is the demand for the construction projects in the first place. Private construction decisions in the macro economy depend on the current performance of the economy. When the economy is thriving, more construction will occur in the private markets. When the economy is in recession, there is much less demand for construction. Construction can help to jump-start the economy during these down times, due to the multiplier effect; but with a recession, there is no demand in the private sector for doing so. Public construction decisions made by the government, however, don't require such demand to be already present. The government instead can choose to "buy" construction projects at a time when the economy isn't producing its own demand, thereby jump-starting the economy and creating the multiplier effect at a time when the economy needs growth and jobs the most.

This is why a recession and slow growth periods are the best times for the government to invest in the nation's infrastructure. Such investment can help to reduce the effects of a recession, increase employment in the private sector, and smooth out the business cycle.

Why a School System Should Not Be Run Like a Business

A successful business is one that maximizes the bottom line. It is successful because it gets the most "bang for the buck". It cuts out wasteful spending, and only spends what is required to achieve its output level. So why not use this model for the school system? Wouldn't it make the taxpayer and the economy better off?

To answer these questions, first take a look at what makes a business successful, and how this success helps the economy.

[Please follow along - this is somewhat lengthy and doesn't get to the part about schools until towards the end, but I believe that this approach is necessary in order to get the point across]

For purposes of understanding, take for example a hypothetical company that produces one product. It doesn't matter too much what that product is. The company makes a product, and it needs to sell that product in order for the business to make any money. So the company needs customers who want the product. The customers, in turn, are people who also want the most "bang for the buck". They have a limited amount of money that can be allocated towards a combination of all the competing uses of their money, including spending it on the product that this company sells. This is a budget constraint for customers. If the company lowers its price, then more people are likely to put the company's product within its budget, and the people who already buy the product might be willing to buy more at the lower price. If the company raises its price, then the opposite would be expected to occur. The business can sell more units at a lower price, fewer units at a higher price. These customers are working on a budget constraint. They can increase the budget, and become consumers of more products, by making more money to add to the budget. So they can make changes in their personal lives to increase their incomes. They can hire themselves out to work for a paycheck. They can do things that make them qualified for higher paying jobs. They become part of a different kind of market, a labor market. This labor market in turn becomes part of the decisions that a company makes when it produces its product.

So the customers will buy more if the price is lower. The business, on the other hand, will make more money if it can sell the same product, at the same cost to the business, if the price is higher. So the business and the customers have competing interests. The business will adjust its price until it finds one that will maximize profits, given the amount that it can sell at different prices. This balances the competing interests of the business and its customers. The price that creates this balance is called the market price. The business can maximize its profits given the level of demand. The customers who want to purchase at the market price will purchase, while others will be "priced out of the market". They voluntarily choose not to purchase at that price. Instead, they simply use their budgets for something else. Nobody gets hurt, nobody feels left out. If the customers really want something that they cannot afford, they can try to find a way to afford it, such as increasing the budget. This also helps the economy, as it increases the size and skills of the labor market.

A business doesn't just compete with "other uses of people's budgets" for its customers. It also competes with other businesses that produce the same product, or a product that is similar enough for customers to consider as a good substitute. If you define "product" in its general usage, then you can see that customers can choose one company's product over another company's product for a variety of reasons. Reasons such as: the price, the quality, the convenience of purchase, how well they know the name of the company, even how pretty the package is. This gives a company a choice as to a "niche" in the market to target. For example, a company that sells women's clothing can choose to produce high-end clothing, using the most famous fashion designers and the most expensive, but highest quality, production methods. Or, it could target any number of other types of customers, each with a different budget and taste. It can then set its production costs according to its target customers.

Once the business finds its target customers, then it can increase its profits by eliminating all wasteful spending. As long as different options are available for the process of providing the product, the company is better off with the lowest-cost of its choices. If it isn't targeting the customers who are buying the latest fashions, it doesn't have to pay for the best fashion designers. If it doesn't require the most expensive materials, the most expensive sewing methods, then it doesn't need to pay for the best materials. It doesn't have to pay for the most skilled workers, or the labor costs (wages and benefits) that the labor markets says the skilled workers will receive (remember that labor is another market, separate from, but related to, the product market). It can use more automated equipment and fewer workers, if that will cut costs and still produce the desired product that meets the specifications of its target customers.

I know, you thought that this was going to be about schools. It is, and I'll get to that shortly. But please keep following along, because understanding these basic points about businesses is important to understanding how businesses are different from schools.

In theory, when a business is successful at this, it helps the economy. That is what capitalism is all about. The workers, the materials, the equipment, even the land, are put to efficient use, producing a product that people want, at a cost that people are willing to pay. Efficiency means success in a capitalistic economy. Even if a company fails, perhaps because it isn't good at cutting costs, or doesn't target its customer base well, or for whatever reason, then that is considered good for the economy in the long run. A failed business means that these resources (workers, material, equipment, land) had not been used efficiently. They are freed up, to be used by another business that finds a customer base to target. Resources get reallocated until somebody finds a more efficient use for them.

This is the business model. There are some important assumptions that are required for this model to work. First of all, you will notice that this model requires that the goal of the business is profit maximization. Nothing else, just maximizing profits. Another important assumption is that whoever pays all the costs associated with a business also receives all the benefits (profits).

That last part requires an explanation. Suppose this business model produces a business that employs a factory that pollutes the air, or the water. This imposes a cost to the neighborhood, perhaps even beyond the neighborhood. The cost doesn't have to be a monetary cost that people pay out of their current budgets, but it could be. Breathing dirty air, looking at a smog-filled scene, having fish in the river downstream dying; these are just some of the costs. If the business doesn't have to pay these costs directly, then these costs are not factored into the decisions about how much of the product to produce, or at what price. If the price isn't affected, then it doesn't factor into the customers' decisions about how much to buy. As a result, too much of something is produced. The added costs are external costs, imposed by the business but paid for by society. When such external costs occur, it doesn't necessarily mean that the company should shut down. It just means that if these costs were added, the company would produce a smaller amount. So the market becomes inefficient by overproducing.

Inefficiency is also created when the business produces something that is beneficial, but the company doesn't get compensated for the benefits; and more people receive the benefits than just the ones who pay for the benefits. For example, a company that produces flu shots will create a public benefit beyond the benefit received by those who pay for the flu shots. The person who receives a flu shot will feel safer from the protection. But even people who don't get the flu shot will receive a degree of benefit from living in a neighborhood with less sickness going around. This "less sickness" is created by other people receiving the flu shots. In the case of an external benefit, the company will produce less than the desired quantity. If it could be compensated for this benefit, it would be willing and able to produce more, and more people would benefit.

The added social costs and benefits discussed here are called externalities.

Ok, now, those are the points that I wanted to make about the business model. Finally, I want to talk about how this all relates to a school system. Remember the assumptions required to make the business model work for society: profit maximization as the only goal of a business, and no externalities. Now, look at what a school system is:

What are the goals of a school system? A wide range of views will answer this question. Should a school be a job factory? Should it prepare everybody for college? Should it promote the arts? Should it create "well-rounded" individuals? Should it prepare individuals for future societal and technological changes that cannot be identified yet? Should it simply teach people to think for themselves? Should it be tailored according to somebody's idea of current needs of society? I have seen many different ideas and I'm sure you have also. In the United States, practical experience by the founders, settlers, and others who followed led to a demand for universal free education. The idea is that the entire society benefits from having everybody educated (an externality). Whatever the goal of education is, it does not mean "profit maximization" as described above on how businesses operate. How do you select a "niche" customer base? You need to cut out all wasteful spending in order to achieve efficiency, but how do you select the quality of the factors of production? How do you decide what level of labor skills to hire? Do you hire from the unskilled labor market, or do you try to get the best? Students are the raw materials, and students are also the finished products. You cannot pick the quality of the raw materials and achieve universal education. You cannot pick the quality of the raw materials and meet the goals of society, unless your goals are to throw away the chance that some kids will have in life. This would mean throwing away entire demographics. It would mean throwing away the American dream of equal opportunity, a chance to be upwardly mobile. Even if you could quantify success (profit) in a way that counts achievement instead of money, you cannot properly account for all of the external benefits that are inherent in the education system. Education is an investment in the future: in our children, in the future of our standard of living. This investment pays off many times over, well into future generations.

This all adds up to: Education is a key part of the nation's infrastructure. It is not a business. It cannot be run successfully using the same approach that businesses use to maximize profits. With external benefits being a key part of the education system, it is society who receives the benefits; the most efficient model is for society to pay the costs.

The quality of the output depends on how you measure the output, on the quality of the resources you put into the system, and dealing with the fact that the system does not choose its own "raw materials", but society does.

I wrote this analysis from the standpoint of an economist using basic concepts of economics. I tried to keep the terminology geared as much as possible towards those who are not economists. I hope I succeeded in making it understandable, but doing it this way made the text quite a bit longer than it would have been otherwise.

Over One Half of All Members of the U.S. Congress Engaged in Un-American Activities

Signers of the Taxpayer Protection Pledge have violated the oath of office and the Constitution.

Can this be classified as treason? You be the judge. But signing the "pledge" is in clear violation of the Constitution and the oath of office for members of Congress who have sworn to uphold the Constitution. The pledge in question, of course, is the Taxpayer Protection Pledge that members of Congress have signed for Grover Norquist's Americans for Tax Reform. Whether treasonous or not, members of Congress who have signed this pledge, at a minimum, should be expelled from Congress for un-American activities.

Here is the proof:

First of all, the pledge that every single member of Congress has taken upon accepting the job:

"I do solemnly swear (or affirm) that I will support and defend the Constitution of the United States against all enemies, foreign and domestic; that I will bear true faith and allegiance to the same; that I take this obligation freely, without any mental reservation or purpose of evasion; and that I will well and faithfully discharge the duties of the office on which I am about to enter: So help me God."

What are these "duties of the office" mentioned in the oath? Article I of the Constitution spells them out in Section 8. The very first one: "The Congress shall have the Power To lay and collect Taxes, Duties, Imposts and Excises, to pay the Debts and provide for the common Defence and general Welfare of the United States..."

Article I, Section 8 then continues with a specific list of duties, all of which require funding. There is nothing in the Constitution or the oath of office that is consistent with allowing a pledge to a private partisan group to take precedence and over-ride the oath of office. On the contrary, such a pledge violates both the Constitution and the oath of office.

As a convenience, I have included the full text of the Constitution in the appendix to this book.

What exactly is the "Taxpayer Protection Pledge"? This is a pledge to serve a specific political agenda regardless of the duties of office, regardless of the national interest. The Constitution requires members of Congress to collect revenue and make expenditures. It does not say that taxes can only go down and never up. The duties of office spelled out in the Constitution require members of Congress to be flexible to meet the needs of the nation according to circumstances as they develop. It is more than short-sighted for members of Congress to decide that circumstances could never develop that would necessitate a tax increase of any kind. It is also a dereliction of duty to not only decide this, but to make a pledge stating that they would never consider a tax increase under any circumstances.

To repeat for emphasis: it is not possible for anybody to know for certain that circumstances would never arise in which the Constitutional duties that members of Congress are sworn to uphold would include the need to increase tax revenues. This impossibility is what makes such a pledge a clear violation of the oath of office, a violation of the Constitution itself.

This is the pledge, the one that violates the Constitution and the oath of office, signed by members of Congress at the request of Grover Norquist:

"I, _____, pledge to the taxpayers of the _____ district of the state of _____, and to the American people that I will:

ONE, oppose any and all efforts to increase the marginal income tax rates for individuals and/or businesses; and

TWO, oppose any net reduction or elimination of deductions and credits, unless matched dollar for dollar by further reducing tax rates."

This is the House version; the Senate version doesn't reference a district but otherwise is identical.

This pledge clearly represents un-American activity for anybody who signs it while under oath of office in Congress, or for anybody who takes the oath of office subsequent to signing this pledge without denouncing the pledge first. But what should be done about violators? Clearly, they are unfit for office and should be removed. Criminal charges seem to be in order. But what process could be used to accomplish what rightfully needs to be done? Who is going to impeach 52% of Congress? Who is going to convict them? Can they be charged with treason?

The answer to the first two questions is that these members of Congress are not going to admit to violating their constitutional duties, let alone impeach and convict themselves. They have indeed violated the Constitution, but does this fact rise to the level of treason?

Here is where the terminology can get sticky. I understand when people call such un-American activity "treason". We are talking about people who would rather trash the U.S. Constitution and the U.S. economy for nothing more than partisan gain, to avoid compromising on a political philosophy. For these people, partisanship is clearly more important than the United States itself; partisanship is more important than the economy and the health and safety of the citizens; partisanship is more important than a sworn oath to protect the Constitution.

This definitely meets some definition of treason, but it might not be enough to get a conviction on a charge of treason. For that, the activity would have to meet the Constitutional standard: "Treason against the United States, shall consist only in levying War against them, or in adhering to their Enemies, giving them Aid and Comfort". [Article III, Section 3]

To me, it would be more useful to avoid using the word treason so that the discussion doesn't go off-track, with everybody arguing over the Constitutional definition instead of the issue at hand. But the activity still is very much un-American and meets the definition of "high crimes".

So, how could these violators receive punishment, given that 52% of the people in charge of punishment are in on the conspiracy? According to the Constitution, the House of Representatives has sole power of impeachment, and the Senate has sole power to try impeachments. And what does it say about the voters of America who elect these people even after they prove in writing that they are violating the Constitution and the oath of office? Many voters are voting for these people in part because they are doing this. What does all of this say about those voters? This isn't the only such violation of these people who are sworn to represent us and uphold the Constitution: some of them are actually on record saying that they wanted the American economy to fail between elections. Many who are not on record saying this are voting along partisan lines with those who are on record - they are all part of the conspiracy. These people need to be removed from office and punished for the violations! But how can that possibly happen when these people are the majority of the insiders?

Those who have violated the Constitution and the oath of office by signing this pledge include many very prominent politicians, including Congressional leaders, people who have run for the office of president, and people who have been mentioned as potential presidential candidates in the future.

Members of Congress Who Have Signed Grover Norquist's Taxpayer Protection Pledge in Violation of the Constitution and the Oath Of Office

This list is based on the 112th Congress, 2011-2012. These are members of the House of Representatives, except for the ones indicated as being members of the Senate.

Alabama:

Jeff Sessions (Senate); Richard Shelby (Senate); Jo Bonner; Martha Roby; Mike Rogers; Robert Alderholt; Mo Brooks; Spencer Bachus

Alaska:

Lisa Murkowski (Senate); Don Young

Arizona:

Jon Kyl (Senate); John McCain (Senate); Paul Gosar; Trent Franks; Ben Quayle; David Schweikert; Jeff Flake

Arkansas:

John Boozman (Senate); Rick Crawford; Tim Griffin; Steve Womack

California:

Wally Herger; Dan Lungren; Tom McClintock; Jeff Denham; Devin Nunes; Kevin McCarthy; Elton Gallegly; Buck Mckeon; David Dreier; Ed Royce; Jerry Lewis; Gary Miller; Ken Calvert; Mary Bono Mack; Dana Rohrabacher; John Campbell; Darrell Issa; Brian Bilbray; Duncan D. Hunter

Colorado:

Scott Tipton; Corey Gardner; Doug Lambom; Mike Coffman

Florida:

Marco Rubio (Senate); Jeff Miller; Steve Southerland; Ander Crenshaw; Richard Nugent; Cliff Stearns; John Mica; Daniel Webster; Gus Bilirakis; Bill Young; Dennis Ross; Vern Buchanan; Connie Mack; Bill Posey; Tom Rooney; Ileana Ros-Lehtinen; Lincoln Diaz-Balart; Allen West; Sandy Adams; David Rivera

Georgia:

Johnny Isakson (Senate); Saxby Chambliss (Senate); Jack Kingston; Lynn Westmoreland; Tom Price; Austin Scott; Tom Graves; Paul Broun; Phil Gingrey

Idaho:

Mike Crapo (Senate); James Risch (Senate); Raul Labrador; Michael Simpson

Illinois:

Mark Kirk (Senate); Peter Roskam; Joe Walsh; Robert Dold; Adam Kinzinger; Judy Biggert; Randy Hultgren; Tim Johnson; Don Manzullo; Bobby Schilling; Aaron Schock; John Shimkus

Indiana:

Dan Coats (Senate); Marlin Stutzman; Todd Rokita; Dan Burton; Mike Pence; Larry Buschon; Todd Young

Iowa:

Tom Latham; Steve King

Kansas:

Jerry Moran (Senate); Pat Roberts (Senate); Tim Huelskamp; Lynn Jenkins; Michael Pompeo

Kentucky:

Mitch McConnell (Senate); Rand Paul (Senate); Ed Whitfield; Brett Guthrie; Geoff Davis; Hal Rogers; Ben Chandler

Louisiana:

David Vitter (Senate); Steve Scalise; Jeffery Landry; John Fleming; Rodney Alexander; Bill Cassidy; Charles Boustany

Maryland:

Andy Harris; Roscoe Bartlett

Massachusetts:

Scott Brown (Senate)

Michigan:

Dan Benishek; Bill Huizenga; Justin Amash; Dave Camp; Fred Upton; Tim Walberg; Mike Rogers; Candice Miller; Thad McCotter

Minnesota:

John Kline; Erik Paulsen; Michele Bachmann; Chip Cravaack

Mississippi:

Roger Wicker (Senate); Alan Nunnelee; Gregg Harper; Steven Palazzo

Missouri:

Roy Blunt (Senate); Todd Akin; Vicky Hartzler; Sam Graves; Billy Long; Jo Ann Emerson; Blaine Luetkemeyer

Montana:

Dennis Rehberg

Nebraska:

Mike Johanns (Senate); Ben Nelson (Senate); Jeff Fortenberry; Lee Terry; Adrian Smith

Nevada:

Dean Heller (Senate); Mark Amodei; Joe Heck

New Hampshire:

Kelly Ayotte (Senate); Frank Guinta; Charlie Bass

New Jersey:

Robert Andrews; Frank LoBiondo; Jon Runyan; Chris Smith; Scott Garrett; Leonard Lance; Rodney Frelinghuysen

New Mexico:

Steve Pearce

New York:

Peter King; Bob Turner; Michael Grimm; Nan Hayworth; Chris Gibson; Ann Marie Buerkle; Tom Reed

North Carolina:

Richard Burr (Senate); Renee Ellmers; Walter Jones Jr.; Virginia Foxx; Howard Coble; Sue Myrick; Patrick McHenry

North Dakota:

Rick Berg

Ohio:

Rob Portman (Senate); Steve Chabot; Jean Schmidt; Mike Turner; Jim Jordan; Bob Latta; Bill Johnson; Steve Austria; John Boehner; Pat Tiberi; Steve LaTourette; Steve Stivers; James Renacci; Bob Gibbs

Oklahoma:

Tom Coburn (Senate); Jim Inhofe; John Sullivan; Frank Lucas; Tom Cole; James Lankford

Oregon:

Greg Walden

Pennsylvania:

Pat Toomey (Senate); Mike Kelly; Glenn Thompson; Jim Gerlach; Pat Meehan; Michael Fitzpatrick; Bill Shuster; Thomas Marino; Lou Barletta; Charlie Dent; Joseph Pitts; Tim Murphy

South Carolina:

Jim DeMint (Senate); Lindsey Graham (Senate); Tim Scott; Joe Wilson; Jeff Duncan; Trey Gowdy; Mick Mulvaney

South Dakota:

John Thune (Senate); Kristi Noem

Tennessee:

Bob Corker (Senate); Lamar Alexander (Senate); Phil Roe; John Duncan; Chuck Fleischman; Scott DesJarlais; Diane Black; Marsha Blackburn; Stephen Fincher

Texas:

John Cornyn (Senate); Kay Bailey Hutchison (Senate); Louie Gohmert; Ted Poe; Sam Johnson; Ralph Hall; Jeb Hensarling; Joe Barton; John Culberson; Kevin Brady; Michael McCaul; Mike Conaway; Kay Granger; Mac Thornberry; Ron Paul; Bill Flores; Randy Neugebauer; Lamar Smith; Pete Olson; Francisco Canseco; Kenny Marchant; Michael Burgess; Blake Farenthold; John Carter; Pete Sessions

Utah:

Michael Lee (Senate); Orrin Hatch (Senate); Rob Bishop; Jason Chaffetz

Virginia:

Scott Rigell; Randy Forbes; Robert Hurt; Bob Goodlatte; Eric Cantor; H. Morgan Griffith

Washington:

Jaime Herrera; Doc Hastings; Cathy McMorris; Dave Reichert

West Virginia:

David McKinley; Shelley Moore Capito

Wisconsin:

Ron Johnson (Senate); Paul Ryan; Jim Sensenbrenner; Tom Petri; Sean Duffy; Reid Ribble

Wyoming:

Mike Enzi (Senate); Cynthia Lummis

Collective Bargaining & Free Market Economics

How does collective bargaining distort free markets?

The simple answer: It does not. Collective bargaining actually enhances the power of free markets to bring about efficiency in the economy. Collective bargaining does not create distorted markets.

Here is how collective bargaining enhances free market efficiency:

First, an overview of how free markets work.

Free markets create efficiency through a process that involves many voluntary transactions. Consumers prefer to pay the lowest price possible for any specific good. Sellers prefer to receive the highest price possible for any specific good, within the framework of their cost structure. Free markets produce the most efficient outcome of price and quantity bought/sold because the process involves finding the price at which the quantity that consumers want to buy matches the quantity that sellers are willing to sell. This is called the equilibrium price. Consumers who demand a price lower than the equilibrium price will voluntarily take themselves out of that market; sellers who demand a price higher than the equilibrium price will take themselves out of that market. Those who are left in the market, both buyers and sellers, will include people who get more than they are willing to settle for: Consumers who would be willing to pay a higher price, and producers who would be willing to sell for a lower price. This creates something called surplus: Consumer surplus is the amount that consumers gain from the difference between the price that they have to pay and the price that they are willing to pay; producer surplus is the difference between the price that sellers receive and the price that they are willing to sell for. The more free the markets, the larger the total surplus (consumer surplus plus producer surplus).

Labor has its own market. The labor market is just like a market for goods and services, except that it is derived. The demand for labor is derived from the demand for the goods and services that labor is hired to produce. In the labor market, the workers are the sellers, the employers are the buyers. The same rules of supply and demand apply to the labor market, but the demand for labor is related to the demand for the product being produced.

Now, here is how collective bargaining fits into the market process:

Truly free markets do not exist in the real world. Varying degrees of free markets exist, but none of them are completely free markets. There are many reasons for this, reasons that comprise a different topic than the purpose of this writing. The point is, truly free markets are only a theoretical concept that involves a number of assumptions that have to hold up; assumptions that cannot be realized in the real world. When these assumptions fail, market failure occurs, with accompanying inefficiencies and market distortions.

The problem with the labor market, without collective bargaining, is that the process of determining the terms of employment are never truly voluntary transactions. Remember from the overview above that free markets are efficient because the transactions are voluntary. In order for transactions to be truly voluntary, one important assumption must hold true: Each party to any transaction must have equal access to information that is relevant to the decisions made regarding potential transactions. This equal access to information is called symmetrical information. Asymmetric information, when one party doesn't share all of the relevant information that it has, is one source of market failure. The existence of this form of market failure is something that a consensus of economists, both conservative and liberal, agrees on.

Without collective bargaining, whether employees face a take-it-or-leave-it offer or can negotiate terms individually, no symmetrical information exists. Employees and potential employees will not know how much they contribute to productivity. They likely won't have complete information regarding the working conditions that they face. This information, at least a truthful version of it, will not be given to individual employees or applicants. Employers will base their decisions on this information, but because of the conflicting goals of buyers and sellers in the labor market, the employers will have an incentive to hide this information from employees. They have no incentive to share exactly what they know, share exactly what information they are basing their decisions on.

Collective bargaining is a process that results in more, not less, information being shared. It results in more, not less, symmetrical information. It results in markets that are more, not less, free.

This has implications in the economy that go far beyond the scope of any individual contract, or any individual market. If more information being shared results in higher wages, more benefits, or better working conditions for employees, then that is an indication that, in the absence of collective bargaining, the employees are being exploited (exploitation being a result of this particular market failure). It means that denying the right to collective bargaining distorts the market; the absence of collective bargaining certainly does not create results that are based on free markets. With labor markets that are distorted in favor of employers at the expense of employees, the markets for goods and services are also distorted. Remember, the demand for labor is derived from the demand for goods and services, and the cost of labor is a cost of providing those gods and services. Labor is part of the household sector of the economy; so are consumers. When distorted markets result in less income for households, the economy ends up producing fewer goods for consumers, fewer opportunities for producers to earn profits.

This is a paradox for employers - individually, they are better off paying employees as little as possible; collectively and ultimately, their profits depend on an economy that is working efficiently, which in turn depends on consumer demand. One of the basic principles of economics is that economists should never commit the fallacy of composition. The fallacy of composition involves taking what is good in an individual case and arguing that it must therefore also be good in the aggregate. Arguing that the economy works better when collective bargaining is not allowed is a fallacy of logic. The economy as a whole depends on the free flow of transactions: Businesses produce goods, consumers buy goods; businesses hire workers, workers spend the income earned on the goods being produced. Consumers demand, producers produce. Consumers get value for their money; businesses earn profits. Market power is shared between the business sector and the household sector, between sellers and buyers. This is the basic model of how a free market economy works.

Anything that takes away from the sharing of market power, by distorting markets, creates a bottleneck in the economy. And then the system breaks down. Proof that we have a problem in our economy is the continual redistribution of wealth. Not wealth that is redistributed to "poor" people, as is popularly claimed, but wealth that is redistributed to the point where the gap between rich and poor grows larger and larger over time, with no letup in the trend. The system has broken down, and will not be fixed until this trend is reversed. The last time the gap between corporate profits and wages has been this large was just prior to the Great Depression. This is a situation that simply is not sustainable, due to a bottleneck in the system.

Some people have heard this argument, focused on the part about more market power for workers and consumers, and called it advocating for socialism. It is nothing of the kind: It is an argument for the markets to be free to do what they are supposed to do. More market power, not less. Market intervention occurs when collective bargaining rights are denied, not when they are allowed. Freedom includes the freedom of collective bargaining.

Contrary to what many people insist, a free market economy does not simply mean giving more and more power to the business sector, or to large corporations. A free market economy depends on a balance between different sectors of the economy. The corporate lobby has duped millions of people into falling for this lie.

This analysis should not be implied as relating to all issues involving unionization. It is limited only to the collective bargaining aspect of unions.

How Big Is Government in the United States?

"Big Government" is a topic that certainly seems to be on everybody's mind these days. It seems like everybody has an opinion about: A bloated government; an over-sized bureaucracy; government workers who are "overpaid and don't produce anything in the economy"; out-of-control spending and high taxes; unsustainable and unmanageable federal deficits; top-heavy government dominated by Washington instead of local jurisdictions.

Most of the opinions seem to be based on things other than actual facts, and on a focus that doesn't include all of the costs and benefits of each facet of government. Facts are certainly available - tons of data are available online from many different sources, including the federal government itself. Sorting through the facts and figures in order to make sense of it all can be very cumbersome.

So what are the real facts? What is the truth, with all of the political rhetoric and interpretations removed? How can all of that data be reduced to something that is easy to understand? I decided to put together just the key numbers that are necessary for seeing the size of the United States government in perspective. More can be learned from sorting through more detailed lists of figures. But for a quick look at the big picture, here is a summary:

For perspective in the numbers, here is the size of the overall economy:

GDP: $15.534 trillion nominal, $15.052 real (2009 base year)

U.S. population: 312 million people

With these numbers in mind for perspective, here are the figures relating to the size of the government:

Total federal spending: $3.6 trillion, which is 24% of real GDP

Total federal deficit: $1.3 trillion, which is 9% of GDP

Federal government revenue comes from the following sources:

Individual income taxes 47%

Payroll taxes (Social Security, Medicare) 36%

Corporate income taxes 8%

Ad valorem taxes 6%

Business taxes and other revenue 4%

(Numbers don't add up to 100% due to rounding)

Federal expenditures fall into the following categories:

Defense spending 24%

Entitlements:

Health Care (Medicare and Federal Medicaid) 24%

Pensions (Social Security) 22%

Unemployment and other entitlements (Welfare) 13%

The above three categories, accounting for 59% of government spending, are collectively known as entitlements; entitlements plus defense spending account for 83% of all federal spending.

Interest on national debt 6%

Education 3%

Transportation 3%

Protection 1%

General government 1%

Other 3%

Those are the dollar figures and percentages relating to the revenue and spending categories. What about the total number of employees?

The federal government employs a total of 2,854,251 civilians, of which 2,619,051 are full-time employees. The total monthly payroll for these employees is $16,118,609,850.

What about state and local governments? How do they stack up against the total population as well as the federal government payrolls?

These figures have been published a little differently. Here is the breakdown for the states, cumulatively:

Full-time employees 3,779,258

Part-time employees 1,534,267

Full-time equivalent (combined full & part time) 4,359,380

Total monthly payroll $19,971,861,990

Here is the same data for local governments cumulatively:

Full-time employees 10,786,166

Part-time employees 3,201,897

Full-time equivalent (combined full & part time) 11,973,790

Total monthly payroll $50,511,637,373

Keep in mind that different levels of government are responsible for different functions. For each of these levels of government (federal, state, local), information on many different categories of workers is available. Instead of showing long lists of these, I have listed the top five categories and their percentages of the total:

Federal civilian employees:

National defense and international relations 28%

Postal services 22%

Hospitals 7%

Police 7%

Natural resources 7%

State government employees:

Higher education 39%

Corrections 11%

Hospitals 9%

Public welfare 5%

Highways 5%

Local government employees:

Elementary & secondary education 56%

Police protection 7%

Hospitals 5%

Higher education 3%

Fire protection 3%

These lists contain only the top five categories for each level of government; the ones listed comprise 73% of what many call "government bureaucracy".

These numbers mean that as a percentage of full-time workers, the federal civilian government makes up 14% of government, state government makes up 23%, and local governments make up 63%.

Notes on these figures:

I used fiscal year 2011 figures for most of this information because 2011 is the last year that many of these figures are available. Putting data together in order to get a picture of size involves using one date instead of using a time frame that includes several different dates. Using one date has the disadvantage of excluding long-term trends and instead includes abnormalities that may not be relevant for long-term analysis. Federal expenditures as a percentage of GDP are abnormally high for 2011 due to consequences of high unemployment and related policies such as automatic stabilizers on both the revenue and expenditure sides.

Postal employees make up 22% of federal employment but are not included in the general budget.

For perspective on the number of government employees, in 2011 the top five private sector employers, in terms of number of global employees:

1. Walmart 2,100,000 employees worldwide

2. IBM 426,751 employees

3. UPS 400,600 employees

4. McDonald's 400,000 employees

5. Target 355,000 employees

Much more information that is relevant to opinions about all of this is available, but beyond the scope of a quick overview. This would include more details than these broad categories, as well as things like a true cost / benefit analysis for each possible policy change. A policy of reducing the size of government in sufficient amounts to make any real difference would necessarily have to take into consideration which specific categories of spending to cut, which specific programs to cut, and which specific jobs to cut.

The term "entitlements" in the categories listed does not mean "government handouts". It simply means that specific recipients are entitled to the money. In most cases, the money is in the form of insurance funds that people pay into specifically so that they will be eligible for benefits later.

Other than that, I leave it up to the reader to interpret these numbers. The sources that I have used include:

http://www.census.gov/govs/apes/

http://www.usgovernmentspending.com/

http://www.measuringworth.com/usgdp/

http://www.money.cnn.com/magazines/fortune500/2011/performers/companies/biggest/employees.html

Oil and Gasoline Prices in the United States: Causes, Consequences, and Policy Implications

This analysis largely applies to both crude oil and gasoline. Some of the statistics presented are based on oil, some on gasoline. Here is a brief summary of the difference between oil prices and gasoline prices:

Oil, in the context of gasoline, refers to crude oil. Crude oil, or unrefined oil, is also known as petroleum. When petroleum is refined, it is converted into a number of petroleum-based products. Each product is sold in a separate set of markets. Some of these products are used as fuel, some are not. The largest share is used for fuel products, and gasoline comprises a large share of the fuel products.

Crude oil and gasoline, therefore, have different markets, and therefore different pricing trends. The pricing trends should be closely related, since crude oil is the major resource used in the production of gasoline, and since gasoline comprises such a large percentage of the uses of crude oil. Still, there will be differences due to changes in demand for each market, changes in inventories, and speculation in the commodities markets.

The differences between oil prices and gasoline prices should not factor into the conclusions presented in this writing.

Crude oil is a commodity that is traded in global markets. The prices are determined by supply and demand in the global economy. The United States produces and supplies 8.91% of the world's oil supply and consumes 22.6% of the global demand. Recent large increases in demand have come from emerging economies such as China and India, but the United States still consumes more than the next three largest oil consumers combined (China, Japan, and India).

Oil prices are very much demand-driven. A recent study by economists at the St. Louis Federal Reserve Bank looked at four components of oil prices: global supply, global demand, inventory demand, and speculation. The study concluded that changes in demand accounted for about 40% of the price changes over the past decade. The second largest contributing factor was speculation at 15%, with changes in inventories the third largest factor, and changes in supply the fourth largest factor.

The changes in demand largely stem from growth in the emerging economies of China and India. The global economic downturn in 2008 accounted for a large decrease in demand.

What about the actual price changes for gasoline in the United States in recent years? If you compare changes in gasoline prices with changes in the CPI index of inflation, you will find that gasoline prices are extremely volatile relative to other prices. Normal inflation (CPI) has been particularly stable in recent years. Prices tend to go up, slowly but in a stable manner. Gasoline prices, on the other hand, have had many wild swings, both up and down. These wild swings have a direct impact on the overall economy.

Another conclusion can be drawn from long term trend in prices. Putting the wild swings aside, the long term trend is upward. Long term, gasoline prices do continue to increase. The rate of increase in the long term trend is similar to the long term trend in overall inflation. Gasoline prices, in the long run, add little to overall inflation. Volatile short term price swings mean that when gasoline prices are rising, they do add to inflation. But when gasoline prices are falling, they tend to be deflationary.

Although long term price trends indicate that gasoline prices are equally as inflationary as other prices in the long run, perhaps they are slightly more inflationary because of a flaw in the measurement of the CPI. The CPI does not take into consideration product improvements, including technological advances. No such upward bias exists in gasoline prices, since gasoline doesn't tend to come in new models every year.

Back to the issue of the price volatility of gasoline, the wild up and down swings. If you look at the price changes in percentage terms, a somewhat regular pattern emerges, with peaks and troughs in gas prices occurring roughly once every quarter. Also, the degree of volatility has apparently diminished somewhat since the beginning of the economic recovery in 2009.

The only obvious abnormality in the pricing trend for gasoline is a very large drop in prices in 2008. That corresponds to the global financial crisis and Great Recession. The world economy collapsed at that time, and global gasoline prices collapsed along with it.

The degree of volatility in gasoline prices increased tremendously with a spike in 1999, and continued through 2008. Since then, volatility has been much lower. What is the cause of this? I don't know, but I believe it is something that needs to be looked into.

What impact does all of this have on the overall economy?

Gasoline prices, and prices of other oil derivatives used for fuel, affect the cost of almost everything. Anything that requires fuel for shipping and / or storage will have cost increases when the price of fuel goes up. On the other hand, they will have cost decreases when the prices go down. The overall, long term trend is that prices for gasoline increase at about the same rate as the average of other prices in the economy. The long term trend probably is not a large factor in the overall economy. The short term volatility, though, means less business and consumer confidence, less risk taking in investments, and therefore less production is likely to occur.

Different classes of individuals and companies will be affected differently, depending on the degree to which they depend on gasoline for their livelihoods. Gasoline tends to be very inelastic (meaning that people will pay a higher price to purchase roughly the same quantity) compared to most products, but some people have demands that are more elastic than other people's demands. When gasoline prices go up more than incomes, consumption of other goods and services decreases. Savings also decrease.

What are the policy implications of gas prices? What can, and should, our politicians do about the problems?

In order to truly deal with the problem, facts must be separated from fiction; reality must be separated from rhetoric. This will not be easy to accomplish, because of the polarized political climate in the United States. Policy positions are being developed on the right and on the left that rely as much on rhetoric as on reality, that appeal to party bases and emotions. What follows here is an attempt to deal with the facts only. It will completely satisfy neither the right nor the left. It will agree with neither party's position on the issue.

What can, and should, policy makers do about the price of gasoline?

Take a look at the top four factors of oil prices, as listed by the St. Louis Fed's economists:

Global supply

Global demand

Oil Inventory demand

Speculation

Global Supply: It has been noted above that the United States produces 8.91% of the world's oil supply, and that prices are determined in a global market. What can policy makers do about this?

Can the United States government increase the global supply of oil, enough to create a significant drop in the global price? To a large extent, oil companies have access to the known oil reserves. They extract what is economically feasible. In order to induce them to drill more, the prices would have to rise, not fall, significantly. A higher price for gasoline would be the cost of a larger supply. This wouldn't solve the price problem, and the higher price necessary would mean a lower standard of living, but it would increase the availability of fossil fuels. The higher price would be an incentive to speed up development of alternative energy sources.

What about concentrating on a large increase in domestic production in order to decrease domestic prices?

The markets would still be global. Any increase in production would have to be large enough to affect the global price. Can, and should, United States policy be designed to accomplish this? As noted above, the United States produces 8.91% of the world's oil supply. But we only have about 1.6% of the world's known oil reserves. We are already drilling a larger percentage of our reserves than the rest of the world. Much of what we have available is already controlled by oil companies, and will only be extracted if the long term price increases significantly, or if technological advances make drilling more economical. The oil reserves that would require additional government approval make up a small amount of known feasible reserves, and cannot possibly be enough to lower the global price significantly. Tapping into this area would require significant compromises regarding the political hot topic of external (environmental) costs.

Just as importantly, the St Louis Fed study found that changes in supply account for a very small portion of changes in price.

The industry is demand driven. The political slogan "drill, baby, drill" is not a reality based solution. It is pure rhetoric that cannot solve our current problems.

What about supply from sources outside the United States? Can the U.S. government influence that? It is worth making every diplomatic attempt to make sure that the fair trade practices are observed, including the prices of exports to the United States. The question then would become, can we do more in this regard than we are already doing? I'm not in a position to give a valid answer to that question. I am not convinced that free trade today is all that free. This is definitely something to look into.

What about completing the controversial Keystone pipeline? Would that significantly decrease domestic prices by increasing domestic and global supply? No, the pipeline would add no significant amount of supply either globally or domestically. It is basically a transportation issue, with the potential to increase the rate of production slightly by increasing the rate of transportation. It would have very little effect on global supplies, and there are significant environmental issues involved.

Global Demand: It has been noted above that the United States consumes by far the largest share of oil, but that increases in demand have come from China and India. However, demand is by far the most significant factor in oil prices. From the standpoint of demand, a significant decrease in demand would be required in order to significantly decrease prices. Since demand is, by far, the largest factor in gasoline prices, a decrease in global demand would be a logical place to look for ways to cut prices.

What could policy makers do in this regard? They could attempt to convince people to cut back on energy use, and at the same time encourage the production of alternative energy sources. Those policies, if successful, would counter the largest cause of higher prices. Economically, this would make sense. However, these ideas have political drawbacks. For example, laws have been passed requiring higher fuel standards and people have been encouraged to demand vehicles with higher fuel mileage – yet these ideas have been scoffed at for being too "liberal". But it cannot be denied that anything that increases demand also increases price. If you choose to consume more energy, you are contributing to increases in energy prices. Some of the loudest complaints about high gasoline prices come from people whose mindset contributes to higher prices.

Oil Inventory Demand: I mention this because it is one of the factors in the pricing of oil. But I have seen no stories, no studies, to indicate that this is an area that needs "corrected". So I will pass on making any suggestions.

Speculation: It has been noted that speculation accounts for about 15% of the price changes in oil. The way that speculation works: investors buy futures contracts in the anticipation of prices increasing in the future. They can turn around and sell these contracts in order to trade them for contracts that go further into the future. This puts upward pressure on current prices as well. When more speculators sell than buy, the prices go back down. It appears that this speculation not only increases prices, but also increases the volatility of prices. The argument for legal speculation usually includes the idea that speculators provide the service of decreasing volatility; it appears that this argument is not valid when it comes to speculating on commodities such as crude oil.

Policy makers can put restrictions on speculation, or pass laws to discourage the activity. But keep in mind, speculation is a relatively small (15%) part of the price equation. Such policy changes may help, but probably not as much as some people (largely left of center politically) would expect.

The bottom line: policies that are designed to increase domestic production will fail to achieve a goal of decreasing gasoline prices.

In order to significantly increase supply, either the price will have to increase significantly or trade needs to be made less "free" and more "fair".

Prices can be decreased with a decrease in demand. There is plenty of leeway in demand to accomplish this economically, but perhaps not politically. It seems that politics is the stumbling block here.

What about a completely different approach? What about the idea of "following the money"? A lot has been made, especially from those on the left end of the political spectrum, about the idea that large profits for oil companies are "obscene" when prices are high and people are suffering as a result. What about taxing these profits?

Taxing oil company profits will not decrease prices. It may or may not increase prices, depending on many factors that are outside the purpose of this writing, but there definitely will be no forces for lower prices unleashed by higher taxes. It is true, however, that oil company profits increase when prices increase. Does that mean that oil companies are responsible for the higher prices? Let's see the proof of that before blaming them. It's also true that oil profits decrease when prices go down. Volatility in prices means that in the long run, oil and gas prices don't go up any more than other prices in the economy. Windfall oil profits exist, but they are only temporary.

Data sources used:

Wikipedia, "List of countries by oil production"

NationMaster.com

www.research.stlouisfed.org

Think You Know The Basics Of Economics And How The Economy Works? Try This Short Quiz...

1. When viewed from the point of view of the overall size of each company, and treating each company's overall output as one market, which market structure does the vast majority of corporations fit into?

   A. perfect competition

   B. monopolistic competition

   C. oligopoly

   D. monopoly

2. Which market structure contains zero corporations?

   A. perfect competition

   B. monopolistic competition

   C. oligopoly

   D. monopoly

3. Rank these components of oil prices from highest to lowest in terms of how much they affect price changes:

   A. supply

   B. demand

   C. speculation

   D. seasonal inventory adjustments

4. In the United States, which answer is closest to the state of the economy from the end of WWII until 1980?

A. The top 1% of income earners received 1% of all income, while the bottom 90% of income earners received 90% of all income.

B. The top 1% of income earners received 10% of all income, while the bottom 90% of income earners received 50% of all income.

C. The top 1% of income earners received 70% of all income, while the bottom 90% of income earners received 10% of all income.

D. The top 1% of income earners received 80% of all income, while the bottom 90% of income earners received 5% of all income.

5. In the United States, which answer is closest to the state of the economy just prior to the Great Recession which began in December, 2007?

A. The top 1% of income earners received 1% of all income, while the bottom 90% of income earners received 90% of all income.

B. The top 1% of income earners received 10% of all income, while the bottom 90% of income earners received 50% of all income.

C. The top 1% of income earners received 70% of all income, while the bottom 90% of income earners received 10% of all income.

D. The top 1% of income earners received 80% of all income, while the bottom 90% of income earners received 5% of all income.

6. The following presidents all served in office for 8 years. During which one's term in office was the government's share of the economy the largest, and mostly increased throughout his 8 years in office?

A. Dwight Eisenhower

B. Ronald Reagan

C. Bill Clinton

D. George W. Bush

7. Which president served while the federal budget deficit decreased 8 consecutive years?

A. Dwight Eisenhower

B. Ronald Reagan

C. Bill Clinton

D. George W. Bush

8. Rank the levels of government in the United States from most to fewest total employees.

A. Federal

B. State

C. Local

9. The Bureau of Labor Statistics, a division of the Department of Labor, publishes the official unemployment rate on a monthly basis. This official rate ignores people who have given up looking for a job, the discouraged workers. It also ignores people who are qualified for work in a skilled position, want to work in such a position, but only work part time in an unskilled job because that is the only kind of job that they can find. People in these two groups are called the "hidden unemployed". Why doesn't the Bureau of Labor Statistics compile the number of hidden employed, and report them along with the "official" unemployed?

10. How does each of the following events, by itself, without assuming specific subsequent events and ignoring any possible

multiplier effects, change the nation's total money supply? Does it create an increase, a decrease, or no change in the money supply?

A. You take all of the change out of your pocket every night, and put it in a piggy bank at home. You figure this money will be used to finance a vacation in 5 years, but you have access to it in case there is an emergency in the meantime.

B. Your paycheck is $3000. On average, you end up taking $300 of this in cash for miscellaneous spending money, put $1,500 into a checking account at your local credit union for other expenditures, put $800 into a savings account at the same credit union, and transfer the remaining $400 to a brokerage account with which you buy shares of foreign stocks on the open market.

C. A mutual funds manager decides to make a change in the diversity of a mutual fund. It sells stocks worth $1,000,000 to a brokerage firm, and buys different stocks worth $1,000,000 from the same broker. The broker receives $20,000 for these transactions, which is deducted from the sales proceeds that the mutual fund manager receives.

D. The same mutual funds manager must pay out $500,000 to various clients who need the money for living expenses. It uses $100,000 from its cash position to finance this transaction, and the remaining $400,000 comes from sales of blue chip stocks to a brokerage firm. It pays the broker $5,000 for this transaction, which is deducted from the fund's cash position.

11. Economics often depends on mathematical equations. Consider two equations, X and Y:

X: $5 + 8 - 6 + 4 = M$

Y: 5 (which is found from a consensus of experts) + 8 (which is the result of calculations using 2-month old estimated data) - 6 (which is the result of calculations using 1-year old data estimated from a specific definition of a term that has more than one definition) + 4 (which is the result of last month's opinion poll with a margin of error of +/- 4%) = N

A. What can be said with certainty about the value of M?

B. What can be said with certainty about the value of N?

C. What can be said with certainty about the equality of X and Y?

Keep your answers in mind, along with the reasons behind the answers, and then compare your answers to mine:

Quiz answers:

1. The answer is C, oligopoly. Some companies compete on different levels, with monopolistic competition being closer to reality than oligopoly on some levels. A case can be made for B as the correct answer. My answer is based on the idea that at the corporate level (think of the big decision-makers at headquarters) corporations will tend to focus on a few large competitors. I also am basing my answer on the idea that the assumption of "many competitors" in the monopolistic competition market structure refers to the same number of competitors in the perfect competition market structure, which is a very difficult characteristic to find in the real world. Monopolies do exist, but in much smaller numbers, especially when you have "no close substitutes" as a necessary assumption.

Additional information:

http://economicsonlinetutor.com/MarketStructures.html

2. The answer is A, perfect competition. But this answer depends on the definitions of the terms, which can be defined in fairly general terms. I base my answers on the idea that according to the characteristics of each market structure, perfectly-competitive markets do not exist in the real world, but the other market structures do. If the market structure doesn't exist, then no corporations can be part of it. I can't picture arguments for saying that one of the other answer choices is the best choice, but if you picked more than one, or none, as the answer, and you based your answer on a rational interpretation of the definitions of the market structures listed, then your answer may also be correct.

Additional information:

http://economicsonlinetutor.com/MarketStructures.html

3. The answer is:

B. Demand

C. Speculation

D. Inventory adjustments

A. Supply

In that order. This is based on a study by the St. Louis Federal Reserve Bank.

Additional information:

http://economicsonlinetutor.com/gasprices.html

4. The answer is C: 70% of all income for the top 1%, and 10% of all income for the bottom 90%. This may surprise many people. These numbers appear to be very top-heavy in terms of income distribution, but they are actually numbers that progressive policies and proposals today are trying to duplicate. They are nothing at all like the outcome of a socialist society. A pure socialist society, in terms of income equality, would look exactly like option A. Option B is only a hypothetical situation, never approached in the real world; Option D is the answer to the next question.

Additional information:

http://economicsonlinetutor.com/conservativeorliberaltest.html

5. The answer is D: 80% of all income for the top 1%, and 5% of all income for the bottom 90%. I rounded these numbers from the actual, which were even more top-heavy. This situation has resulted in a smaller middle class, less buying power for the masses of buyers, and inadequate demand throughout the economy. What may look like a relatively small difference in percentage terms, compared to the answer to the previous question, has made a big difference in the performance of the economy. Neither of the real-world sets of

numbers, represented by answer choices C and D, come anywhere near what socialism looks like (choice A). Economic policies that have been proposed as economic fixes to the current state of the economy also look nothing like the socialist outcome of option A.

Additional information:

http://economicsonlinetutor.com/conservativeorliberaltestansw ers.html

6. The answer is B, Ronald Reagan. I included this question here because the correct answer runs counter to the rhetoric of the time, and especially because false claims are being made about this by political candidates as well as by advocates on the airways and all over the internet.

Additional information:

http://economicsonlinetutor.com/useconomichistory.html

7. The answer is C, Bill Clinton. This one is also included because it runs counter to the rhetoric and the stereotypes.

Additional information:

http://economicsonlinetutor.com/useconomichistory.html

8. The answer is, in order:

C. Local

B. State

A. Federal

This may or may not surprise a lot of people, but it will probably surprise some people who listen mostly to rhetoric. Keep in mind that different levels of government tend to have different functions that require different types of workers. This is important when you consider the flow of the money, and the tendency for unfunded mandates (effective ones as well as overt ones) to flow down from higher levels of government, and the different types of funding that is available to each level of government.

Additional information:

http://economicsonlinetutor.com/biggovernment.html

9. This is a trick question, because the answer is that those statistics ARE compiled along with the official unemployment statistics, and are reported at the same time in the same news release. It's just that the media and the commentators tend to focus on the "official" numbers. Those official numbers are also the ones that are most often used by economists for various purposes. There is a reason why the hidden unemployment statistics are kept separate from the official unemployment numbers - if people are not actively looking for a job, they are not likely to find one; and this truth holds regardless of the state of the economy. There is plenty of blame to go around for this confusion, though. The media can be blamed for focusing on the official unemployment rate, and relegating the other, arguably equally important numbers, to being buried in the stories. The public can be blamed for a short attention span that allows this to happen. Economists can be blamed for using the official rate, not only when it is the appropriate number to use, but also when it is the most convenient number available. And the government perhaps can be blamed for using misleading terminology to begin with.

One more misleading aspect of unemployment statistics, not part of this question but it often comes up in discussions: the official employment statistics, whether the official unemployment rate or the other numbers that are published, have absolutely nothing to do with the number of people who are filing for unemployment benefits, or the people whose benefits have run out. You would expect a strong positive correlation, but the compilation of unemployment rate statistics is not based on the statistics relating to unemployment benefits. Those numbers are reported separately, by different groups of people, for different reasons. They don't even cover the same time frame: statistics relating to the unemployment rate are compiled monthly, while statistics relating to claims for benefits are compiled weekly.

Additional information:

http://economicsonlinetutor.com/unemploymentstatistics.html

http://www.bls.gov/home.htm

10. The first thing you should have done, before attempting to answer the specific questions here, is say to yourself something like "wait, this question is too vague to answer. It requires more information, or at least I will have to make some assumptions to go along with the questions before they can be answered!" The intent of this question was to get people to note that there are different definitions for what is counted in the nation's money supply, and the very definition of money itself can become blurry in specific situations. The specific answers to specific parts of this, I don't really care about because that is not the intent of this exercise. The point is that you can answer these questions only if you make some assumptions about what definitions to use. I think this is important to understand, because so many economic models, and so many study results, depend on which specific definitions are being used for money. This is important when calculations are being made for the size of the money supply, for the velocity of money, etc. Personally, I don't trust mathematical conclusions that are based on vague concepts for the calculations. Too many people, including political pundits but also economists, draw conclusions based on assumptions with no apparent realization that such assumptions are being made, and without analyzing the effects of the assumptions on the conclusions.

Here is a small example of what I am talking about: The scenarios depicted in this question involve "money" transactions for different groups: brokerage firms; mutual funds managers; people who are saving money from their paychecks; people who are spending money on normal expenses which aren't specified but would include things like groceries, house payments, and credit card bills; people who are cashing in mutual fund shares to pay for living expenses, perhaps in their retirement years. All of these different types of transactions will affect macro calculations in different ways. They represent different marginal propensities to consume. If you are counting income, and using one MPC figure, individual transactions will be wrong because a broker account will hardly affect consumption at all, while cashing in mutual fund shares as depicted here will go towards consumption. Money multipliers also are affected in different ways. Putting money in a piggy bank won't multiply the nation's money supply the same way that money in a commercial bank could; in fact it can be argued that "piggy bank money" is money taken out of circulation altogether and should not be counted. Instead of multiplying, perhaps you should subtract. But it all depends on the definitions of terms that you are using. I like to think of the "real economy" as what goes on between buyers and sellers of the things that get produced in the economy, the real goods and services as opposed to what goes on in financial transactions. This means that money that is being used solely within the financial industry - say rich people trading existing stocks back and forth among other rich people for potential gains, with no intention of ever cashing in to spend on consumption goods - is something that I would not count in the "real economy". But it does get counted, depending on the definitions that you use. It gets counted, but can distort any resulting calculations based on the magnitudes of the money supply, money velocity, and a multiplier effect.

Additional information:

http://economicsonlinetutor.com/MoneyDefined.html

11. The answer to A is that M = 11. That is the only conclusion that can be drawn with mathematical certainty from these equations. You cannot say with certainty what the value of N would be, because its value is based on several different estimates, and other calculations that don't necessarily use numbers that are consistent with each other. If you know the value of M, but not the value of N, then you cannot simply say that M = N.

This question does have a specific point to make. I see this all the time in economics: People calculate something that would be the equivalent of calculating N in this exercise, and then they turn around and insist that they have just calculated M, with all of its certainty. Many people, economists included, insist that N is equal to M by mathematical definition. After all, both equations, X and Y, are identical mathematically. The problem is that when you say that the results have to be equal, you are saying things like 5 = 5ish by definition, which of course it isn't. The lesson to be learned from this question: You should beware of claims about outcomes of economic policy when the claims state with certainty that the results are "mathematical facts". I have found that more often than not, such claims are saying the same thing as "N = M" in this exercise.

This quiz isn't just testing your ability to find specific answers to specific questions. Some of the questions are designed to do just that. But other questions are designed to see if you can use an "economic thinking" process to arrive at answers.

Are You a Conservative or a Liberal When it Comes to Economic Policy? A Capitalist or a Socialist? Take This Simple Test

What kind of society would we have if all of the income were shared equally among everybody? Would it be okay to share everything equally, even if it meant that individuals would have no incentive to work? What would be the expected result in terms of a standard of living?

What kind of society would we have if all of the income went to 1% of the population, and everybody else got nothing? Would it be okay to let only a few people at the very top earn everything while everybody else starved? If you decide that "those who receive it are the ones who earn it, so it is fair to let them keep it", would you still be in favor of letting 99% of the population go without any income? Would that still be okay? What kind of a standard of living would result?

Believe it or not, policies dictate the end result in terms of income distribution. Even if it isn't your goal, whenever you choose to support a specific set of policies, you are actually choosing to support a specific outcome in terms of income distribution throughout the economy. So, think about which policies that you actually support. If you know that these policies will result in a specific income distribution, which kind of end result, which distribution, would be best for society? Look at the natural outcome as the goal of the policies, because that is what the policies amount to.

Which outcome, in terms of income distribution, do you think would be associated with policies that create the best possible society? I'm not talking about "best possible society" in terms of some kind of a consensus, but simply "best possible society" according to your own personal standards?

No matter which policies you support; no matter if you call yourself a liberal or conservative; a socialist or a capitalist; or something else, the true test is the end result of the policies. With that in mind, take a look at these four different hypothetical income distributions, and then answer the questions that follow. Your answers will determine if you actually support the policies that are associated with the political and economic labels that you claim for yourself. Don't peek at the analysis of the answers before you finish answering the questions, because there is a very strong possibility that your answer will be swayed by the analysis. Be honest with yourself.

A. A: The top 1% of the population receives 1% of all income; the next 4% receive 4% of all income; the next 5% receive 5% of all income; and the bottom 90% receives 90% of all income.

B. The top 1% of the population receives 10% of all income; the next 4% receive 20% of all income; the next 5% receive 20% of all income; and the bottom 90% receives 50% of all income.

C. The top 1% of the population receives 70% of all income; the next 4% receive 10% of all income; the next 5% receive 10% of all income; and the bottom 90% receives 10% of all income.

D. The top 1% of the population receives 82% of all income; the next 4% receive 7% of all income; the next 5% receive 7% of all income; and the bottom 90% receives 4% of all income.

Now, try to answer these questions regarding the four options listed above:

1. Which of the four options is most likely to produce long term stability?

2. Which of these four options is most likely to produce long term growth and increase the standard of living throughout the economy?

3. Which of these four options is most fair?

4. Which of these four options would be a natural end result of policies that you support?

In order to help you decide, here are some points that you might want to consider. Those at the very top are mostly people like hedge fund managers, corporate CEOs, and people born into wealthy families. The bottom 90% includes almost all of the labor force (the working class), the entire middle class, the entire lower class, welfare recipients, almost all small business owners, and most corporate middle managers.

Individuals who are higher up on the income scale will have more money available to invest in businesses in the economy. These same individuals also are much more likely to park their money outside of the economy, such as investments in foreign companies and bank accounts. Higher-income individuals are more likely to make decisions based on tax consequences.

Lower-income individuals are more likely to spend the income that they have on goods and services that are produced in the economy. These individuals will have less discretionary income available for savings and investment.

The upper class is an investor class (not necessarily investing in the domestic economy); the lower class is a consumer class (including consumption from income such as welfare payments and unemployment compensation) and a working class. The middle class is a diverse class that includes savers, investors, small business owners, and the bulk of both consumption and the labor force provided in the economy.

Lower-income individuals will spend a higher percentage of total income on consumption. Higher-income individuals will save or invest a higher the percentage of total income.

Taking the above information into consideration, along with any other information that you believe to be relevant, answer the three questions above with one of the four options in the table. That is the test to determine where you stand on the conservative-to-liberal scale and the capitalist-to-socialist scale (if you have answered honestly).

There is no right or wrong answer. Once you have your choices, keep in mind the reasons behind your choices. Then, check your answers against the following analysis.

Analysis of the Answers

Do you have your answers and the reasons for your choices? Okay, here is an explanation of what this could mean, along with a few words about what your answers say about your position on the conservative-to-liberal and the capitalist-to-socialist scales.

Option A is a strict socialist outcome. The income is equal across all groups. No real difference in income distribution exists. There really is no upper class or lower class in terms of current income. In cases where there are different classes based on previously-accumulated wealth, those distinctions would gradually disappear over time. This is what the numbers would look like if income were distributed equally among everybody in the population.

If you picked option A for your answer to question 4, you are a strict socialist. Not the "mixed economy" advocate of some socialist policies, but a strict socialist based on economic outcome. You aren't interested in equal opportunity, but in equal outcome. The same is true if you picked option A for your answer to question 2, although in that case, you would be basing your answers on socialist theory, and you will be at odds with anybody who advocates for a market-based economy. Market based economics relies on assumptions of incentives and market efficiencies to produce economic growth and increases in the standard of living. If you picked option A for your answer to question 3, then that only says that you consider equal outcome to be "fair". That is totally a judgment call.

Option B is an interesting hypothetical situation. Nothing like it has ever been approached in the United States' economic history, and I know of no policies, conservative or liberal, that are designed to achieve such an outcome. Option B is extremely liberal compared to any economic policies or outcomes that we have ever seen in the USA. To me, it appears to be an outcome that would occur if policy makers took a liberal stance towards possible market failures, and created a market economy with a government that actively worked to fix all such market failures. It appears to me to be a situation where buyers have as much market power as sellers, which is a more true market economy than anything produced by policies or theories. It would be ideal for short term growth. However, it might not be sustainable in the long run. There would need to be a balance between the supply and demand of loanable funds in the long run, and I'm not sure that this scenario would create such a balance.

Since this scenario is strictly hypothetical, any analysis, including my own in the above paragraph, would be theoretical. If you answered Option B for any of the four questions, your answers could theoretically be right in terms of producing stability, or growth, or fairness.

However, based on where this scenario looks compared to actual policies and outcomes that we have for comparison, if you answered Option B for any of the four questions, this would undoubtedly mark you as an economic liberal. You would be towards the extreme liberal side of the conservative-to-liberal scale, and the theory behind your reasons would determine where you stand on the capitalist-to-socialist scale.

Option C is not really hypothetical. It is roughly where the United States economy stood continuously from the time that statistics have been available (around 100 years ago) up until 1980. The top income brackets gained much more than the other income brackets, but all income brackets gained in a relatively constant proportion. This is an outcome that you would expect in a capitalist system that rewards risk and investment, entrepreneurship, yet at the same time pays workers for gains in productivity. The gap between the have and the have-nots is wide, but upward mobility is increasingly a reality.

This is a historical situation of a capitalist economy; there is nothing socialist about it at all. If you picked Option C as your answer to any of the four questions, then you would fall squarely in the capitalist end of the capitalist-to-socialist scale.

This is also the type of outcome that liberals want to return to. Liberal policies in the United States are designed to move policy back towards this type of outcome, based on the idea that such an outcome has historically worked better for everyone. All gained, not just those at the very top. Workers were paid according to productivity, and workers became buying consumers who kept the economy moving. The labor force participation rate was smaller during this time, for the most part, than any time since. Typical households had more real income with one income earner than today's households which often have two income earners. Income tax policies were much more progressive than today (between 1936 and 1980, the marginal tax rates for top income earners ranged from 70% to 94%, compared to 28% to 50% between 1982 and 2013), which helped to offset other types of taxes, which are largely regressive. If you picked option C for the answer to any of the four questions, you are squarely in the liberal end of the conservative-to-liberal scale.

Option C puts you squarely in both the liberal and capitalist camps. There is no truth to the rhetoric that liberal economic policies of today are socialist. Liberal policies of today are actually designed to return partially to the capitalist policies in existence for much of our economic history, when the outcome mirrored the results seen in Option C.

If you picked Option C for the answer to any of the three questions, then that would put you squarely in the liberal and the capitalist ends of the scales. Not extremist in either case, but in those camps.

Option D also is not really hypothetical. It is roughly what the United States economy looked like just before the economy crashed in 2008. The difference between the numbers in Option C and Option D is the cumulative effect of trickle-down economic policies in effect since 1981. Since 1981, the economy has moved from looking like Option C to looking like Option D. Even with a deep recession and a slow but significant recovery, it still looks more like Option D than Option C.

Since both Option C and Option D represent results taken directly from the American economy, let's take a closer look at the differences and similarities. The differences and similarities in the historical record say something about the outcomes of policies, both historical policies and current partisan proposals. Notice that the difference between Option C and Option D is that the top has gained a significant share of the total income, while all the other groups have lost shares. All income growth is now staying at the top. During this time period, productivity has increased tremendously, due in part to technological advances. Classical theory would suggest that workers would be compensated with income gains to match the gains in productivity. But that clearly has not happened. Trickle-down economics has not trickled down. As a result, buying power has decreased, and the top earners are either sitting on their gains (they have no reason to invest in the economy if nobody has buying power), investing in financial instruments that create economic bubbles instead of jobs, or they are investing in foreign countries. Top earners put more effort into loopholes to avoid taxes than in investing in domestic jobs. Statistically, upward mobility has decreased, not increased.

The conservative policies of today are designed not only to maintain the changes in the numbers from Option C (reality before 1981) to Option D (reality since 1981), but also to increase the share of gains going to the very top. This is done in the name of free market capitalism, under the false notion that giving those at the top what they want, at the expense of everybody else, somehow increases the influence of free markets. That is the rhetoric that we are being fed; the reality is that a balance between buyer and seller, with both sides having equal market power, is what a true free market is all about.

If you picked Option D for the answer to any of the four questions, that puts you clearly in the camp of conservative and capitalist. But there are serious questions about whether such an outcome can be considered stable in the long term (that's what many of today's protests are all about) and whether such an outcome can maximize growth in the long term (history shows that austerity is incompatible with growth, and that market power in the hands of one side of the buyer/seller relationship at the expense of the other side is also incompatible with long term growth). There are many obvious objections to the fairness of such a system.

My guess is that many people who consider themselves strict conservatives would have picked one of the options that is not conservative at all. If so, I would respond to these people by saying that the test is completely accurate (it is based entirely on United States economic history and basic economic concepts), but many people who consider themselves to be strict conservatives only choose specific conservative polices whenever they are given their talking points from conservative pundits. When forced to think for themselves, they will often choose something else entirely. Since many of the truths behind these four options are not part of the conservative pundits' talking points, many conservatives will have to think for themselves when taking this test.

Feel free to share this test with your friends who are advocates of both sides of the political spectrum. It would be interesting to see if their results match their rhetoric.

One Change to Corporate Tax Rates Could Create Jobs and Economic Growth

This is my idea for a workable economic plan.

My plan is different from any others that I have seen proposed. It has one main point, a simple point that I believe will improve many aspects of the economy.

The central idea behind my plan, the main piece of my proposal, is this: Make one change to the tax code: Change the corporate tax rate to zero. A zero rate on corporate taxes, but with an important stipulation: the zero rate will only apply to net income up to the amount of a corporation's payroll expense for U.S. based, non-executive personnel. For net income above that amount, a normal corporate tax rate will be applicable.

I believe this simple change to the tax code will work wonders for the economy, both short term and long term. I have it worded so that the zero-tax bracket for corporations applies to 100% of domestic, non-executive payroll expenses. Perhaps studies will show that 100% is not the best percentage to use. Perhaps 50%, or even 150%, or whatever will work better. The main point of my idea is that corporate taxes be based on a percentage of such expenses. The entire idea should not be scrapped if the only thing found wrong with it is the use of 100% as the cut-off point for corporate taxes.

I have a couple of other parts to my plan, parts that may be more difficult to implement, but this change in the corporate tax code is the central idea in my plan. I believe that this one idea can stand alone in terms of improving the economy, regardless of whether other policy changes are implemented or not.

I want to mention the other parts of my plan, but first I want to explain in more detail why I think that this one point, changing the corporate tax rate, will not only improve the economy but also be politically workable.

If corporations have a zero tax rate on net incomes that do not exceed the payroll expenses on their "regular" stateside employees, then it doesn't matter whether or not you agree with the economic theory that these corporations are "job creators" who will create jobs if their taxes are lowered. That theory is based on assumptions about the incentives that are built into free market economics. This change will make that point irrelevant. It doesn't rely on any incentives that are implicit in the theory. Instead, it will actually create these incentives in the real world. No philosophy or theory is needed to believe that this will work. The incentives explicitly become a part of the policy. If they work, the economy is improved. If not, then they will prove the theory wrong. I believe that they will work in a very large way. Yet it doesn't overly complicate the tax code, or include specific laws that have "social engineering" as a goal. Only one target is involved, and it is a general one that doesn't require a detailed plan: give corporations an incentive to invest more in the people of America. This plan does not involve telling corporations how to run their business in order to achieve social goals. Instead, it provides incentives for them to help the economy while keeping their own private goals of profit maximization.

This policy will not raise anybody's tax rates. There is no violation of any philosophy to not raise taxes of any kind. On the contrary, there will be a reduction in effective tax rates. In fact, it can eliminate one source of taxation that has been controversial throughout our history. Corporations will have a legal means, and a huge incentive, to not pay any corporate taxes. This will satisfy those who argue that corporate taxes are "double taxation" or that corporate taxes are simply passed on to consumers in the form of higher prices.

This will change the relative cost of production in favor of domestic production. More exports, fewer imports. This will make the issue of repatriation a smaller issue. This will be an added incentive for corporate goals and strategies to be more in line with national goals and what is best for the overall economy. This would be a change in the right direction for those who believe that the overall economy, as well as specific classes of individuals, suffers because of corporate greed. The imbalance in the economy created by a widening wealth gap will begin to be restored. It will create an incentive to not only hire more workers, but also to pay a living wage. More consumer income, more consumer confidence, and more consumer demand will result. More consumer demand and a new method to explicitly and legally avoid corporate taxes create more business confidence. A deep recession can be avoided, deflation can be avoided, and a lost decade can be avoided.

Short term, we are a long way from an overheated economy; but long term, this will open up the economy for policies that are designed to deal with that situation to become more effective. I have ideas for that as well, but that is a different topic for another day.

Businesses in the United States already deduct wages and payroll expenses from earnings in order to calculate taxable income. They already do not have to pay income taxes on salaries. What this will do is in effect give them a double write-off for expenses relating to non-executive employees. This will change incentives towards paying labor according to productivity, something that has not been occurring in the past 30 years. This will change incentives away from foreign labor and towards domestic labor. More domestic labor that is paid according to productivity will equate to higher domestic demand and economic growth.

This plan will increase government revenue and decrease deficit spending. More people will have enough income to move into the taxpaying brackets. More individual taxpayers will move up into higher tax brackets. The income tax burden will be spread around more, which should satisfy those who believe that the tax burden is unfairly top-heavy. This will also reverse the trend towards a shrinking middle-class. It will put more disposable income in the hands of those who are most likely to spend it in the "real" economy. This should satisfy many liberals.

This simple change is actually a radical departure from anything that has come before. It is a plan that accepts different economic philosophies, different political positions, but doesn't rely on one philosophy "winning" and other philosophies "losing" in the political battle for acceptance. Different economic theories are based on assumptions of how specific policies affect the incentives that in turn affect the health of the overall economy. Different philosophies have dominated policy at different times throughout American history. I have the key numbers that indicate the results of economic policies (see "further reading" below), but these real-world numbers do not change many people's philosophy. With a very complex economy, and room to both interpret the results and hand-pick which data to emphasize, there is very little about the raw data that will change many minds. People simply ignore the numbers, or interpret them in ways that fit their own philosophies. The result: Every policy proposal that is based on a particular philosophy must survive attacks from other philosophies, and survive hardline positions from partisan elected officials. The failure of the Congressional Deficit Panel is a case in point.

This plan would require a carefully worded definition of what constitutes "non-executive" employee compensation. Otherwise, it could be defeated with widespread use of loopholes.

I have no delusions that such a plan will win universal approval. I am just saying that I believe that it can gain enough of a consensus to be workable. There is a portion of the population that will oppose any workable plan. For example, this plan could win over conservatives that believe in conservative principles as being the best tools for creating a healthy economy. But there are other conservatives who believe in conservative principles not as tools for economic gain, but rather as an end in and of themselves - a "starve the beast" attitude displayed by people who would prefer a failing economy if it means "smaller government" - with "smaller government" defined as elimination of all transfer payments. This plan will not satisfy people in that category, because it does not involve a decrease in government revenues. Those who believe that the government spends only because it has access to funds will not like this plan - they will oppose any plan that increases government revenue, even if the only source of such revenue is an increase in economic activity and economic growth. I believe that if such a plan were proposed, those who are against economic growth from a broader income base would be forced to reveal their true motives. Then, let the voters decide.

I mentioned at the beginning of this commentary that my plan had other points that would be more difficult to implement. I want to mention these points at the end because I believe the change in the corporate tax structure discussed above would be sufficient to vastly improve the economy all by itself. It does not rely on other policy changes in order to be effective. At the same time, I believe these other parts of my plan would also have a tremendous positive impact on the long term health of the economy.

Two of these points are unique in the sense that I haven't seen anybody else propose them - they are my ideas alone as far as I know. They are:

1. Change the reporting requirement for publicly-owned corporations to include, clearly visible, the ratio of total CEO compensation to the average beginning salary within the corporation.

2. Require all American publicly-owned corporations that have foreign facilities to be listed on a separate stock exchange.

These two changes do not directly involve a distribution of money, or any payments. They are only non-monetary methods of information dissemination. I believe that people, and in this case, corporate leaders, are likely to respond to non-monetary incentives as well as monetary ones. Potential investors, customers, and the general public will become more aware of just how well corporate behavior is consistent with sound macroeconomic policy. Without telling corporations how to run their businesses, or expecting corporations to stray from their own missions, I believe these changes will mean that more corporations will change their behavior to be more in line with social goals.

Besides the changes listed above, I also believe that other ideas will improve the economy. These other ideas are not my own, and are already part of the public discussion. The fact that they have not been implemented means that they are politically controversial. I cannot add anything to the discussion of these issues, other than to state which ones I support, which include:

Elimination of tax loopholes for wealthy individuals and corporations; an income tax bracket for very high incomes; elimination of favorable tax treatment for capital gains (or at least some form of this - I would suggest two possibilities: either having separate rates for investment income that is from direct business investment and investment income that only creates economic bubbles for existing financial investments; or requiring all taxpayers to pay income taxes on at least half of their incomes at the personal tax rates even if the income is from investments); reversal of the Citizens United decision.

Further reading:

http://economicsonlinetutor.com/useconomichistory.html

Church and State: The Founding Fathers in Their Own Words

What did the Founding Fathers have to say about the separation of church and state?

Did they intend for the United States to be a "Christian nation" based on "Christian (or Judeo-Christian) values"?

Did they even hold religious views compatible with the views that fundamentalists are currently attempting to codify into law?

You be the judge. Included here are many quotes from the founders on the following subjects:

- Religion and the law, especially in terms of the separation of church and state

- Christianity (and its various denominations), Judaism, and even Islam

- Personal views on religion

The quotes listed here are all sourced and verified. I have included none of the many false quotes that have been circulating around the internet. With the standard of only including verified and relevant quotes, I have managed to include quotes from the following founders: Thomas Jefferson (the most widely quoted of them all, and it seems the most widely misquoted as well); James Madison; George Washington; John Adams; Benjamin Franklin; Samuel Adams; and for good measure, one from William Penn.

First of all, misconceptions abound regarding what the Constitution says about Christianity, God, and religion.

The writing of the Constitution took place in 1787 at the Constitutional Convention in Philadelphia. The delegates to the Convention drew upon their experiences with Great Britain, state constitutions, and their study of the history of government. Many of these men were students and advocates of the Enlightenment. They did indeed believe in the virtues of education, general knowledge, scientific advancements, and practicality in government. But did they believe in religion as a guiding principle for government? Here is the entirety of what the original Constitution says about religion:

"no religious Test shall ever be required as a Qualification to any Office or public Trust under the United States." Article VI, United States Constitution.

That's it. That is the entirety of what the Founders deemed necessary to include in the Constitution regarding religion. There is no mention of any deity, and there is no passage that can be construed to indicate a preference for one religion or type of religion within government. This is certainly not consistent with many of today's claims, and much of today's political rhetoric.

What about the Bill of Rights, and the rest of the amendments? The entire text from the amendments regarding religion can be found at the very beginning of the First Amendment in the Bill of Rights:

"Congress shall make no law respecting an establishment of religion"

Nothing exists in the entire document, including all of the amendments, about the United States being a Christian nation. What the Constitution does say about religion does not support such a claim.

When I point this out, I hear things like, "yeah, but they put all of that in the Declaration of Independence. That document is loaded with many references to Christianity and makes it clear that we are to be a Christian nation." Really? The Declaration of Independence makes exactly four references of appeal to a singular higher power, none of which is in the same context as today's rhetoric about the United States as a Christian nation. Here they are, word for word:

- "the separate and equal station to which the Laws of Nature and of Nature's God entitle them"

- "We hold these truths to be self-evident, that all men are created equal, that they are endowed by their Creator with certain unalienable Rights"

- "appealing to the Supreme Judge of the world for the rectitude of our intentions"

- "And for the support of this Declaration, with a firm reliance on the protection of Divine Providence"

Those four references are the only mentions of God in the Declaration of Independence; so much for the notion that it is loaded with proof that they created a Christian nation.

As a convenience, I have included the full texts of the Declaration of Independence and the Constitution (with amendments) in the appendix to this book.

Now, let's move on to other words from the founders. The Declaration of Independence was penned by Thomas Jefferson. He is the most widely quoted of the Founders on the subject of religion and government. I have included quotes from Jefferson on the subject of the separation of church and state, as well as many on the subject of his personal religious beliefs, so that they can be compared to the views of those who want to impose some sort of religious laws on the citizens of the United States.

The quotes begin here:

"I am for freedom of religion, & against all maneuvres to bring about a legal ascendancy of one sect over another."

-Thomas Jefferson, Letter to Elbridge Gerry (1799).

"Believing with you that religion is a matter which lies solely between man and his God, that he owes account to none other for his faith or his worship, that the legislative powers of government reach actions only, and not opinions, I contemplate with sovereign reverence that act of the whole American people which declared that their legislature should "make no law respecting an establishment of religion, or prohibiting the free exercise thereof," thus building a wall of separation between church and State."

-Thomas Jefferson, Letter to Danbury Baptist Association, CT. (1 January 1802). This statement is the origin of the often used phrase "separation of Church and State".

"Christianity neither is, nor ever was, a part of the common law."

-Thomas Jefferson, Vol. 1 Whether Christianity is Part of the Common Law (1764). Published in The Works of Thomas Jefferson in Twelve Volumes, Federal Edition, Paul Leicester Ford, ed., New York: G. P. Putnam's Sons, 1904, p. 459.

"Religion & Govt. will both exist in greater purity, the less they are mixed together."

-James Madison, Letter to Edward Livingston (1822-07-10).

"The Pennsylvania legislature, who, on a proposition to make the belief in God a necessary qualification for office, rejected it by a great majority, although assuredly there was not a single atheist in their body. And you remember to have heard, that when the act for religious freedom was before the Virginia Assembly, a motion to insert the name of Jesus Christ before the phrase, "the author of our holy religion," which stood in the bill, was rejected, although that was the creed of a great majority of them."

-Thomas Jefferson, Letter to Albert Gallatin (16 June 1817). Published in The Works of Thomas Jefferson in Twelve Volumes, Federal Edition, Paul Leicester Ford, ed., New York: G. P. Putnam's Sons, 1904, Vol. 12, p. 73.

"Besides the danger of a direct mixture of religion and civil government, there is an evil which ought to be guarded against in the indefinite accumulation of property from the capacity of holding it in perpetuity by ecclesiastical corporations. The establishment of the chaplainship in Congress is a palpable violation of equal rights as well as of Constitutional principles. The danger of silent accumulations and encroachments by ecclesiastical bodies has not sufficiently engaged attention in the U.S."

-James Madison, "Monopolies, Perpetuities, Corporations, Ecclesiastical Endowments" an essay probably written sometime between 1817 and 1832. It has sometimes been incorrectly portrayed as having been uncompleted notes written sometime around 1789 while opposing the bill to establish the office of Congressional Chaplain. It was first published as "Aspects of Monopoly One Hundred Years Ago" in 1914 by Harper's Magazine and later in "Madison's Detached Memoranda" by Elizabeth Fleet in William and Mary Quarterly (1946).

"The Citizens of the United States of America have a right to applaud themselves for giving to Mankind examples of an enlarged and liberal policy: a policy worthy of imitation. All possess alike liberty of conscience and immunities of citizenship. It is now no more that toleration is spoken of, as if it was by the indulgence of one class of people that another enjoyed the exercise of their inherent natural rights. For

happily the Government of the United States, which gives to
bigotry no sanction, to persecution no assistance, requires only
that they who live under its protection should demean
themselves as good citizens in giving it on all occasions their
effectual support. May the Children of the Stock of Abraham,
who dwell in this land, continue to merit and enjoy the good
will of the other Inhabitants; while every one shall sit under his
own vine and fig tree, and there shall be none to make him
afraid."

-George Washington, Letter to the Hebrew Congregation of
Newport, Rhode Island (1790).

"The Religion then of every man must be left to the conviction
and conscience of every man; and it is the right of every man to
exercise it as these may dictate.

"Who does not see that the same authority which can establish
Christianity, in exclusion of all other Religions, may establish
with the same ease any particular sect of Christians, in
exclusion of all other Sects? that the same authority which can
force a citizen to contribute three pence only of his property for
the support of any one establishment, may force him to
conform to any other establishment in all cases whatsoever?

"We hold it for a fundamental and undeniable truth, 'that
Religion or the duty which we owe to our Creator and the
Manner of discharging it, can be directed only by reason and
conviction, not by force or violence.' The Religion then of
every man must be left to the conviction and conscience of
every man; and it is the right of every man to exercise it as
these may dictate. This right is in its nature an unalienable
right. It is unalienable; because the opinions of men, depending
only on the evidence contemplated by their own minds, cannot
follow the dictates of other men: It is unalienable also; because
what is here a right towards men, is a duty towards the Creator.
It is the duty of every man to render to the Creator such

homage, and such only, as he believes to be acceptable to him. This duty is precedent both in order of time and degree of obligation, to the claims of Civil Society. Before any man can be considered as a member of Civil Society, he must be considered as a subject of the Governor of the Universe: And if a member of Civil Society, who enters into any subordinate Association, must always do it with a reservation of his duty to the general authority; much more must every man who becomes a member of any particular Civil Society, do it with a saving of his allegiance to the Universal Sovereign. We maintain therefore that in matters of Religion, no man's right is abridged by the institution of Civil Society, and that Religion is wholly exempt from its cognizance. True it is, that no other rule exists, by which any question which may divide a Society, can be ultimately determined, but the will of the majority; but it is also true, that the majority may trespass on the rights of the minority.

"The free men of America did not wait till usurped power had strengthened itself by exercise, and entangled the question in precedents. They saw all the consequences in the principle, and they avoided the consequences by denying the principle. We revere this lesson too much soon to forget it. Who does not see that the same authority which can establish Christianity, in exclusion of all other Religions, may establish with the same ease any particular sect of Christians, in exclusion of all other Sects? that the same authority which can force a citizen to contribute three pence only of his property for the support of any one establishment, may force him to conform to any other establishment in all cases whatsoever?

"It is moreover to weaken in those who profess this Religion a pious confidence in its innate excellence and the patronage of its Author; and to foster in those who still reject it, a suspicion that its friends are too conscious of its fallacies to trust it to its own merits.

"During almost fifteen centuries has the legal establishment of Christianity been on trial. What have been its fruits? More or less in all places, pride and indolence in the Clergy, ignorance and servility in the laity, in both, superstition, bigotry and persecution.

"What influence in fact have ecclesiastical establishments had on Civil Society? In some instances they have been seen to erect a spiritual tyranny on the ruins of the Civil authority; in many instances they have been seen upholding the thrones of political tyranny: in no instance have they been seen the guardians of the liberties of the people. Rulers who wished to subvert the public liberty, may have found an established Clergy convenient auxiliaries. A just Government instituted to secure & perpetuate it needs them not.

"[A]ttempts to enforce by legal sanctions, acts obnoxious to go great a proportion of Citizens, tend to enervate the laws in general, and to slacken the bands of Society. If it be difficult to execute any law which is not generally deemed necessary or salutary, what must be the case, where it is deemed invalid and dangerous?

"And what may be the effect of so striking an example of impotency in the Government, on its general authority?

"Because finally, "the equal right of every citizen to the free exercise of his religion according to the dictates of conscience" is held by the same tenure with all his other rights. If we recur to its origin, it is equally the gift of nature; if we weigh its importance, it cannot be less dear to us; if we consider the "Declaration of those rights which pertain to the good people of Virginia, as the basis and foundation of government," it is enumerated with equal solemnity, or rather studied emphasis. [Often misquoted as "Religion is the basis and foundation of government."]

"We the Subscribers say, that the General Assembly of this Commonwealth have no such authority: And that no effort may be omitted on our part against so dangerous an usurpation, we oppose to it, this remonstrance; earnestly praying, as we are in duty bound, that the Supreme Lawgiver of the Universe, by illuminating those to whom it is addressed, may on the one hand, turn their Councils from every act which would affront his holy prerogative, or violate the trust committed to them: and on the other, guide them into every measure which may be worthy of his [blessing, may re]dound to their own praise, and may establish more firmly the liberties, the prosperity and the happiness of the Commonwealth."

-James Madison, "Memorial and Remonstrance Against Religious Assessments" (1785), opposing a "Bill establishing a provision for Teachers of the Christian Religion".

"We have abundant reason to rejoice, that, in this land, the light of truth and reason has triumphed over the power of bigotry and superstition, and that every person may here worship God according to the dictates of his own heart. In this enlightened age, & in this land of equal liberty, it is our boast, that a man's religious tenets will not forfeit the protection of the laws, nor deprive him of the right of attaining & holding the highest offices that are known in the United States.

"Your prayers for my present and future felicity are received with gratitude; and I sincerely wish, Gentlemen, that you may in your social and individual capacities taste those blessings, which a gracious God bestows upon the righteous."

-George Washington, Letter to the the members of The New Church in Baltimore (22 January 1793), published in The Writings Of George Washington (1835) by Jared Sparks, p. 201.

"Let us with caution indulge the supposition, that morality can be maintained without religion. Whatever may be conceded to the influence of refined education on minds of peculiar structure, reason and experience both forbid us to expect, that national morality can prevail in exclusion of religious principle."

-George Washington, Farewell Address.

"We think ourselves possessed, or, at least, we boast that we are so, of liberty of conscience on all subjects, and of the right of free inquiry and private judgment in all cases, and yet how far are we from these exalted privileges in fact! There exists, I believe, throughout the whole Christian world, a law which makes it blasphemy to deny or doubt the divine inspiration of all the books of the Old and New Testaments, from Genesis to Revelations. In most countries of Europe it is punished by fire at the stake, or the rack, or the wheel. In England itself it is punished by boring through the tongue with a poker. In America it is not better; even in our own Massachusetts, which I believe, upon the whole, is as temperate and moderate in religious zeal as most of the States, a law was made in the latter end of the last century, repealing the cruel punishments of the former laws, but substituting fine and imprisonment upon all those blasphemers upon any book of the Old Testament or New. Now, what free inquiry, when a writer must surely encounter the risk of fine or imprisonment for adducing any argument for investigating into the divine authority of those books? Who would run the risk of translating Dupuis? But I cannot enlarge upon this subject, though I have it much at heart. I think such laws a great embarrassment, great obstructions to the improvement of the human mind. Books that cannot bear examination, certainly ought not to be established as divine inspiration by penal laws. It is true, few persons appear desirous to put such laws in execution, and it is also true that some few persons are hardy enough to venture to depart from them. But as long as they continue in force as laws, the human mind must make an awkward and clumsy progress in its investigations. I wish they were repealed. The substance and essence of Christianity, as I understand it, is eternal and unchangeable, and will bear examination forever, but it has been mixed with extraneous ingredients, which I think will not bear examination, and they ought to be separated."

-John Adams, Letter to Thomas Jefferson (23 January 1825), published in Letters: The Complete Correspondence Between Thomas Jefferson and Abigail and John Adams (UNC Press, 1988), p. 607.

"As to Jesus of Nazareth, my Opinion of whom you particularly desire, I think the System of Morals and his Religion, as he left them to us, the best the world ever saw or is likely to see; but I apprehend it has received various corrupt changes, and I have, with most of the present Dissenters in England, some Doubts as to his divinity; tho' it is a question I do not dogmatize upon, having never studied it, and I think it needless to busy myself with it now, when I expect soon an Opportunity of knowing the Truth with less Trouble."

-Benjamin Franklin, As quoted in Benjamin Franklin: An Exploration of a Life of Science and Service (1938) by Carl Van Doren, p. 777.

"In regard to religion, mutual toleration in the different professions thereof is what all good and candid minds in all ages have ever practised, and, both by precept and example, inculcated on mankind."

-Samuel Adams, The Rights of the Colonists (1772).

"All persons shall have full and free liberty of religious opinion; nor shall any be compelled to frequent or maintain any religious institution."

-Thomas Jefferson, Draft Constitution for Virginia (June 1776).

"All men have a natural and indefeasible right to worship Almighty God according to the dictates of their own consciences; no man can of right be compelled to attend, erect, or support any place of worship, or to maintain any ministry against his consent; no human authority can, in any case whatever, control or interfere with the rights of conscience, and no preference shall ever be given by law to any religious establishment or modes of worship."

-William Penn, Declaration of Rights.

"In the middle ages of Christianity opposition to the State opinions was hushed. The consequence was, Christianity became loaded with all the Romish follies. Nothing but free argument, raillery & even ridicule will preserve the purity of religion."

-Thomas Jefferson, Notes on Religion (October 1776), published in The Works of Thomas Jefferson in Twelve Volumes, Federal Edition, Paul Leicester Ford, ed., New York: G. P. Putnam's Sons, 1904, Vol. 2, p. 256.

This is by no means an exhaustive list of quotes available from the Founders expressing similar sentiments. Not convinced yet? Or perhaps you would like to see more for reference and study. Here are some more quotes from Thomas Jefferson:

"Locke denies toleration to those who entertain opinions contrary to those moral rules necessary for the preservation of society; as for instance, that faith is not to be kept with those of another persuasion, ... that dominion is founded in grace, or who will not own & teach the duty of tolerating all men in matters of religion, or who deny the existence of a god (it was a great thing to go so far—as he himself says of the parliament who framed the act of toleration ... He says 'neither Pagan nor

Mahomedan nor Jew ought to be excluded from the civil rights of the Commonwealth because of his religion.' Shall we suffer a Pagan to deal with us and not suffer him to pray to his god? Why have Christians been distinguished above all people who have ever lived, for persecutions? Is it because it is the genius of their religion? No, its genius is the reverse. It is the refusing toleration to those of a different opinion which has produced all the bustles and wars on account of religion. It was the misfortune of mankind that during the darker centuries the Christian priests following their ambition and avarice combining with the magistrate to divide the spoils of the people, could establish the notion that schismatics might be ousted of their possessions & destroyed. This notion we have not yet cleared ourselves from."

-Thomas Jefferson, Notes on Religion (October, 1776). Published in The Works of Thomas Jefferson in Twelve Volumes, Federal Edition, Paul Leicester Ford, ed., New York: G. P. Putnam's Sons, 1904, Vol. 2, pp. 267.

"Difference of opinion is advantageous in religion. The several sects perform the office of a Censor morum over each other. Is uniformity attainable? Millions of innocent men, women, and children, since the introduction of Christianity, have been burnt, tortured, fined, imprisoned; yet we have not advanced one inch towards uniformity. What has been the effect of coercion? To make one half the world fools, and the other half hypocrites. To support roguery and error all over the earth. Let us reflect that it is inhabited by a thousand millions of people. That these profess probably a thousand different systems of religion. That ours is but one of that thousand. That if there be but one right, and ours that one, we should wish to see the 999 wandering sects gathered into the fold of truth. But against such a majority we cannot effect this by force. Reason and persuasion are the only practicable instruments. To make way for these, free enquiry must be indulged; and how can we wish others to indulge it while we refuse it ourselves?"

-Thomas Jefferson, Query XVII, Notes on the State of Virginia.

"Compulsion in religion is distinguished peculiarly from compulsion in every other thing. I may grow rich by art I am compelled to follow, I may recover health by medicines I am compelled to take against my own judgment, but I cannot be saved by a worship I disbelieve & abhor."

-Thomas Jefferson, Notes on Religion (October 1776), published in The Works of Thomas Jefferson in Twelve Volumes, Federal Edition, Paul Leicester Ford, ed., New York: G. P. Putnam's Sons, 1904, Vol. 2, p. 266.

"But those facts in the Bible which contradict the laws of nature, must be examined with more care, and under a variety of faces. Here you must recur to the pretensions of the writer to inspiration from God. Examine upon what evidence his pretensions are founded, and whether that evidence is so strong, as that its falsehood would be more improbable than a change in the laws of nature, in the case he relates. For example in the book of Joshua we are told the sun stood still several hours. Were we to read that fact in Livy or Tacitus we should class it with their showers of blood, speaking of statues, beasts, etc. But it is said that the writer of that book was inspired. Examine therefore candidly what evidence there is of his having been inspired. The pretension is entitled to your inquiry, because millions believe it. On the other hand you are astronomer enough to know how contrary it is to the law of nature that a body revolving on its axis as the earth does, should have stopped, should not by that sudden stoppage have prostrated animals, trees, buildings, and should after a certain time have resumed its revolution, & that without a second general prostration. Is this arrest of the earth's motion, or the evidence which affirms it, most within the law of probabilities?"

-Thomas Jefferson, Letter to his nephew Peter Carr from Paris, France, (10 August 1787). Published in The Works of Thomas Jefferson in Twelve Volumes, Federal Edition, Paul Leicester Ford, ed., New York: G. P. Putnam's Sons, 1904, Vol. 5, pp. 324-327.

"Truth will do well enough if left to shift for herself. She seldom has received much aid from the power of great men to whom she is rarely known & seldom welcome. She has no need of force to procure entrance into the minds of men. Error indeed has often prevailed by the assistance of power or force. Truth is the proper & sufficient antagonist to error."

-Thomas Jefferson, Notes on Religion (October 1776), published in The Writings of Thomas Jefferson : 1816-1826 (1899) edited by Paul Leicester Ford, v. 2, p. 102.

"To the corruptions of Christianity I am indeed opposed; but not to the genuine precepts of Jesus himself. I am a Christian, in the only sense he wished any one to be; sincerely attached to his doctrines, in preference to all others; ascribing to himself every human excellence; & believing he never claimed any other."

-Thomas Jefferson, Letter to Benjamin Rush (12 April 1803).

"I never will, by any word or act, bow to the shrine of intolerance, or admit a right of inquiry into the religious opinions of others."

-Thomas Jefferson, Letter to Edward Dowse (19 April 1803).

"Yours is one of the few lives precious to mankind, and for the continuance of which every thinking man is solicitous. Bigots may be an exception. What an effort, my dear sir, of bigotry in politics and religion have we gone through! The barbarians really flattered themselves they should be able to bring back the times of Vandalism, when ignorance put everything into the hands of power and priestcraft. All advances in science were proscribed as innovations. They pretended to praise and encourage education, but it was to be the education of our ancestors. We were to look backwards, not forwards, for improvement … This was the real ground of all the attacks on you. Those who live by mystery & charlatanerie, fearing you would render them useless by simplifying the Christian philosophy — the most sublime and benevolent, but most perverted system that ever shone on man — endeavored to crush your well-earned & well-deserved fame."

-Thomas Jefferson, Letter to Dr. Joseph Priestley (21 March 1801); published in The Life of Thomas Jefferson (1871) by Henry Stephens Randall, Vol. 2, p. 644; this seems to be the source of a misleading abbreviation: "[Christianity is] the most ... perverted system that ever shone on man".

"When the clergy addressed General Washington on his departure from the government, it was observed in their consultation that he had never on any occasion said a word to the public which showed a belief in the Christian religion and they thought they should so pen their address as to force him at length to declare publicly whether he was a Christian or not. They did so. However [Dr. Rush] observed the old fox was too cunning for them. He answered every article of their address particularly except that, which he passed over without notice. Rush observes he never did say a word on the subject in any of his public papers except in his valedictory letter to the Governors of the states when he resigned his commission in the army, wherein he speaks of the benign influence of the Christian religion. I know that Gouverneur Morris, who pretended to be in his secrets & believed himself to be so, has often told me that General Washington believed no more of that system than he himself did."

-Thomas Jefferson, The Anas (February 1, 1800). Published in The Works of Thomas Jefferson in Twelve Volumes, Federal Edition, Paul Leicester Ford, ed., New York: G. P. Putnam's Sons, 1904, Vol. 1, pp. 352–353.

"My religious reading has long been confined to the moral branch of religion, which is the same in all religions; while in that branch which consists of dogmas, all differ[.]"

-Thomas Jefferson, Letter to Thomas Leiper (11 January 1809). Published in The Works of Thomas Jefferson in Twelve Volumes, Federal Edition, Paul Leicester Ford, ed., New York: G. P. Putnam's Sons, 1904, Vol. 11, pp. 89.

"Religion is a subject on which I have ever been most scrupulously reserved. I have considered it as a matter between every man and his Maker in which no other, and far less the public, had a right to intermeddle."

-Thomas Jefferson, Letter to Richard Rush (1813).

"It is between fifty and sixty years since I read it, and I then considered it merely the ravings of a maniac, no more worthy nor capable of explanation than the incoherences of our own nightly dreams. … what has no meaning admits no explanation."

-Thomas Jefferson, Letter to General Alexander Smyth, on the book of Revelation (or The Apocalypse of St. John the Divine) (17 January 1825).

"Well aware that the opinions and belief of men depend not on their own will, but follow involuntarily the evidence proposed to their minds; that Almighty God hath created the mind free, and manifested his supreme will that free it shall remain by making it altogether insusceptible of restraint; that all attempts to influence it by temporal punishments, or burthens, or by civil incapacitations, tend only to beget habits of hypocrisy and meanness, and are a departure from the plan of the holy author of our religion, who being lord both of body and mind, yet choose not to propagate it by coercions on either, as was in his Almighty power to do, but to exalt it by its influence on reason alone; that the impious presumption of legislature and ruler, civil as well as ecclesiastical, who, being themselves but fallible and uninspired men, have assumed dominion over the faith of others, setting up their own opinions and modes of thinking as the only true and infallible, and as such endeavoring to impose them on others, hath established and maintained false religions over the greatest part of the world and through all time: That to compel a man to furnish contributions of money for the propagation of opinions which he disbelieves and abhors, is sinful and tyrannical; ... that our civil rights have no dependence on our religious opinions, any more than our opinions in physics or geometry; and therefore the proscribing any citizen as unworthy the public confidence by laying upon him an incapacity of being called to offices of trust or emolument, unless he profess or renounce this or that religions opinion, is depriving him injudiciously of those privileges and advantages to which, in common with his fellow-citizens, he has a natural right; that it tends also to corrupt the principles of that very religion it is meant to encourage, by bribing with a monopoly of worldly honours and emolumerits, those who will externally profess and conform to it; that though indeed these are criminals who do not withstand such temptation, yet neither are those innocent who lay the bait in their way; that the opinions of men are not the object of civil government, nor under its jurisdiction; that to suffer the civil magistrate to intrude his powers into the field of opinion and to restrain the profession or propagation of principles on supposition of their ill tendency is a dangerous fallacy, which at once destroys all religious liberty, … and finally, that truth is great and will prevail if left to herself; that she is the proper and sufficient antagonist to error, and has nothing to fear from the conflict unless by human interposition disarmed of her natural weapons, free argument and debate ; errors ceasing to be dangerous when it is permitted freely to contradict them."

-Thomas Jefferson, A Bill for Establishing Religious Freedom, Chapter 82 (1779). Published in The Works of Thomas Jefferson in Twelve Volumes, Federal Edition, Paul Leicester Ford, ed., New York: G. P. Putnam's Sons, 1904, Vol. 1, pp. 438–441.

"What an effort, my dear sir, of bigotry in politics and religion have we gone through! The barbarians really flattered themselves they should be able to bring back the times of Vandalism... They believe that any portion of power confided to me, will be exerted in opposition to their schemes. And they believe rightly; for I have sworn upon the altar of god eternal hostility against every form of tyranny over the mind of man. But this is all they have to fear from me: and enough, too, in their opinion."

-Thomas Jefferson, On members of the clergy who sought to establish some form of "official" Christianity in the U.S. government. Letter to Dr. Benjamin Rush (23 September 1800). This has commonly been quoted as "I have sworn upon the altar of God Eternal, hostility against every form of tyranny over the mind of man", "I have sworn upon the altar of God eternal hostility against every form of tyranny over the mind of man", and "I have sworn upon the altar of God, eternal hostility against every form of tyranny over the mind of man." Neither capitalization of "god" and "eternal", nor a comma before or after "eternal" are apparent in the original. The first portion of this statement has also been widely paraphrased as "The clergy believe that any power confided in me will be exerted in opposition to their schemes, and they believe rightly."

"He who steadily observes the moral precepts in which all religions concur, will never be questioned at the gates of heaven as to the dogmas in which they all differ."

-Thomas Jefferson, Letter to William Canby (18 September 1813).

"History, I believe, furnishes no example of a priest-ridden people maintaining a free civil government. This marks the lowest grade of ignorance of which their civil as well as religious leaders will always avail themselves for their own purposes."

-Thomas Jefferson, Letter to Alexander von Humboldt (6 December 1813).

"The priests of the different religious sects, who dread the advance of science as witches do the approach of day-light; and scowl on it the fatal harbinger announcing the subversion of the duperies on which they live. In this the Presbyterian clergy take the lead. the tocsin is sounded in all their pulpits, and the first alarm denounced is against the particular creed of Doctr. Cooper; and as impudently denounced as if they really knew what it is."

-Thomas Jefferson, Letter to José Correia da Serra (11 April 1820).

"Where the preamble declares, that coercion is a departure from the plan of the holy author of our religion, an amendment was proposed by inserting "Jesus Christ," so that it would read "A departure from the plan of Jesus Christ, the holy author of our religion;" the insertion was rejected by the great majority, in proof that they meant to comprehend, within the mantle of its protection, the Jew and the Gentile, the Christian and Mohammedan, the Hindoo and Infidel of every denomination."

-Thomas Jefferson, Autobiography (1821), in reference to the Virginia Act for Religious Freedom.

"The truth is, that the greatest enemies of the doctrine of Jesus are those, calling themselves the expositors of them, who have perverted them to the structure of a system of fancy absolutely incomprehensible, and without any foundation in his genuine words. And the day will come when the mystical generation of Jesus, by the supreme being as his father in the womb of a virgin will be classed with the fable of the generation of Minerva in the brain of Jupiter ... But may we hope that the dawn of reason and freedom of thought in these United States will do away with this artificial scaffolding, and restore to us the primitive and genuine doctrines of this most venerated reformer of human errors."

-Thomas Jefferson, Letter to John Adams (11 April 1823) (Scan at The Library of Congress).

"The whole history of these books is so defective and doubtful that it seems vain to attempt minute enquiry into it: and such tricks have been played with their text, and with the texts of other books relating to them, that we have a right, from that cause, to entertain much doubt what parts of them are genuine. In the New Testament there is internal evidence that parts of it have proceeded from an extraordinary man; and that other parts are of the fabric of very inferior minds. It is as easy to separate those parts, as to pick out diamonds from dunghills."

-Thomas Jefferson, Letter to John Adams, on Christian scriptures (24 January 1814).

"His parentage was obscure; his condition poor; his education null; his natural endowments great; his life correct and innocent: he was meek, benevolent, patient, firm, disinterested, & of the sublimest eloquence.

The disadvantages under which his doctrines appear are remarkable.

1. Like Socrates & Epictetus, he wrote nothing himself.

2. But he had not, like them, a Xenophon or an Arrian to write for him. On the contrary, all the learned of his country, entrenched in its power and riches, were opposed to him, lest his labors should undermine their advantages; and the committing to writing his life & doctrines fell on the most unlettered & ignorant men; who wrote, too, from memory, & not till long after the transactions had passed.

3. According to the ordinary fate of those who attempt to enlighten and reform mankind, he fell an early victim to the jealousy & combination of the altar and the throne, at about 33. years of age, his reason having not yet attained the maximum of its energy, nor the course of his preaching, which was but of 3. years at most, presented occasions for developing a complete system of morals.

4. Hence the doctrines which he really delivered were defective as a whole, and fragments only of what he did deliver have come to us mutilated, misstated, & often unintelligible.

5. They have been still more disfigured by the corruptions of schismatising followers, who have found an interest in sophisticating & perverting the simple doctrines he taught by engrafting on them the mysticisms of a Grecian sophist, frittering them into subtleties, & obscuring them with jargon, until they have caused good men to reject the whole in disgust, & to view Jesus himself as an impostor.

Notwithstanding these disadvantages, a system of morals is presented to us, which, if filled up in the true style and spirit of the rich fragments he left us, would be the most perfect and sublime that has ever been taught by man.

The question of his being a member of the Godhead, or in direct communication with it, claimed for him by some of his followers, and denied by others, is foreign to the present view, which is merely an estimate of the intrinsic merit of his doctrines.

1. He corrected the Deism of the Jews, confirming them in their belief of one only God, and giving them juster notions of his attributes and government.

2. His moral doctrines, relating to kindred & friends, were more pure & perfect than those of the most correct of the philosophers, and greatly more so than those of the Jews; and they went far beyond both in inculcating universal philanthropy, not only to kindred and friends, to neighbors and countrymen, but to all mankind, gathering all into one family, under the bonds of love, charity, peace, common wants and common aids. A development of this head will evince the peculiar superiority of the system of Jesus over all others.

3. The precepts of philosophy, & of the Hebrew code, laid hold of actions only. He pushed his scrutinies into the heart of man; erected his tribunal in the region of his thoughts, and purified the waters at the fountain head.

4. He taught, emphatically, the doctrines of a future state, which was either doubted, or disbelieved by the Jews; and wielded it with efficacy, as an important incentive, supplementary to the other motives to moral conduct."

-Thomas Jefferson, "Syllabus of an Estimate of the Merit of the Doctrines of Jesus, Compared with Those of Others" in a letter to Benjamin Rush (12 April 1803). Published in The Works of Thomas Jefferson in Twelve Volumes, Federal Edition, Paul Leicester Ford, ed., New York: G. P. Putnam's Sons, 1904, Vol. 9 Works Vol. 9 (PDF), pp. 462.

"I may say Christianity itself divided into its thousands also, who are disputing, anathematizing and where the laws permit burning and torturing one another for abstractions which no one of them understand, and which are indeed beyond the comprehension of the human mind[.]"

-Thomas Jefferson, Letter to George Logan (12 November 1816). Published in The Works of Thomas Jefferson in Twelve Volumes, Federal Edition, Paul Leicester Ford, ed., New York: G. P. Putnam's Sons, 1904, Vol. 12, pp. 43.

"The result of your fifty or sixty years of religious reading in the four words: 'Be just and good,' is that in which all our enquiries must end."

-Thomas Jefferson, Letter to John Adams (11 January 1817).

Finally, here is one on the Jefferson Bible. If you don't know what the Jefferson Bible is, Jefferson literally cut up the Gospels, deleted the parts that didn't match his personal beliefs, and repasted the ones he believed in. His beliefs in this regard centered on the idea that Jesus' moral teaching alone was the true gospel; and that the miracles, virgin birth, divinity of Christ, resurrection, etc. were all false teachings added by scribes.

"I, too, have made a wee-little book from the same materials, which I call the Philosophy of Jesus; it is a paradigma of his doctrines, made by cutting the texts out of the book, and arranging them on the pages of a blank book, in a certain order of time or subject. A more beautiful or precious morsel of ethics I have never seen; it is a document in proof that I am a real Christian, that is to say, a disciple of the doctrines of Jesus, very different from the Platonists, who call me infidel and themselves Christians and preachers of the gospel, while they draw all their characteristic dogmas from what its author never said nor saw. They have compounded from the heathen mysteries a system beyond the comprehension of man, of which the great reformer of the vicious ethics and deism of the Jews, were he to return on earth, would not recognize one feature."

-Thomas Jefferson, Letter to Charles Thomson (9 January 1816), on his The Life and Morals of Jesus of Nazareth (the "Jefferson Bible"), which omits all Biblical passages asserting Jesus' virgin birth, miracles, divinity, and resurrection. Published in The Works of Thomas Jefferson in Twelve Volumes, Federal Edition, Paul Leicester Ford, ed., New York: G. P. Putnam's Sons, 1904, Vol. 11, pp. 498–499.

The Founders clearly intended to establish a nation free from government advocacy of any religion. They received their "values" from many sources, some Christian and some not. They believed that religious matters were deeply personal and government had no role to play. They were not unanimous in their personal religious views, and many of these personal views differed widely from those that many people want to impose on us today through legislation.

The Founding Fathers believed that both religion and government would be stronger with a complete separation of the two.

The concept of the separation of church and state has been present from the beginning.

Appendix

The Declaration of Independence

IN CONGRESS, JULY 4, 1776

The unanimous Declaration of the thirteen united States of America

When in the Course of human events it becomes necessary for one people to dissolve the political bands which have connected them with another and to assume among the powers of the earth, the separate and equal station to which the Laws of Nature and of Nature's God entitle them, a decent respect to the opinions of mankind requires that they should declare the causes which impel them to the separation.

We hold these truths to be self-evident, that all men are created equal, that they are endowed by their Creator with certain unalienable Rights, that among these are Life, Liberty and the pursuit of Happiness. — That to secure these rights, Governments are instituted among Men, deriving their just powers from the consent of the governed, — That whenever any Form of Government becomes destructive of these ends, it is the Right of the People to alter or to abolish it, and to institute new Government, laying its foundation on such principles and organizing its powers in such form, as to them shall seem most likely to effect their Safety and Happiness. Prudence, indeed, will dictate that Governments long established should not be changed for light and transient causes; and accordingly all experience hath shewn that mankind are more disposed to suffer, while evils are sufferable than to right themselves by abolishing the forms to which they are accustomed. But when a long train of abuses and usurpations, pursuing invariably the same Object evinces a design to reduce them under absolute Despotism, it is their right, it is their duty, to throw off such Government, and to provide new Guards for their future security. — Such has been the patient sufferance of these Colonies; and such is now the necessity which constrains them to alter their former Systems of Government. The history of the present King of Great Britain is a history of repeated injuries and usurpations, all having in direct object the establishment of an absolute Tyranny over these States. To prove this, let Facts be submitted to a candid world.

He has refused his Assent to Laws, the most wholesome and necessary for the public good.

He has forbidden his Governors to pass Laws of immediate and pressing importance, unless suspended in their operation till his Assent should be obtained; and when so suspended, he has utterly neglected to attend to them.

He has refused to pass other Laws for the accommodation of large districts of people, unless those people would relinquish the right of Representation in the Legislature, a right inestimable to them and formidable to tyrants only.

He has called together legislative bodies at places unusual, uncomfortable, and distant from the depository of their Public Records, for the sole purpose of fatiguing them into compliance with his measures.

He has dissolved Representative Houses repeatedly, for opposing with manly firmness his invasions on the rights of the people.

He has refused for a long time, after such dissolutions, to cause others to be elected, whereby the Legislative Powers, incapable of Annihilation, have returned to the People at large for their exercise; the State remaining in the mean time exposed to all the dangers of invasion from without, and convulsions within.

He has endeavoured to prevent the population of these States; for that purpose obstructing the Laws for Naturalization of Foreigners; refusing to pass others to encourage their migrations hither, and raising the conditions of new Appropriations of Lands.

He has obstructed the Administration of Justice by refusing his Assent to Laws for establishing Judiciary Powers.

He has made Judges dependent on his Will alone for the tenure of their offices, and the amount and payment of their salaries.

He has erected a multitude of New Offices, and sent hither swarms of Officers to harass our people and eat out their substance.

He has kept among us, in times of peace, Standing Armies without the Consent of our legislatures.

He has affected to render the Military independent of and superior to the Civil Power.

He has combined with others to subject us to a jurisdiction foreign to our constitution, and unacknowledged by our laws; giving his Assent to their Acts of pretended Legislation:

For quartering large bodies of armed troops among us:

For protecting them, by a mock Trial from punishment for any Murders which they should commit on the Inhabitants of these States:

For cutting off our Trade with all parts of the world:

For imposing Taxes on us without our Consent:

For depriving us in many cases, of the benefit of Trial by Jury:

For transporting us beyond Seas to be tried for pretended offences:

For abolishing the free System of English Laws in a neighbouring Province, establishing therein an Arbitrary government, and enlarging its Boundaries so as to render it at once an example and fit instrument for introducing the same absolute rule into these Colonies

For taking away our Charters, abolishing our most valuable Laws and altering fundamentally the Forms of our Governments:

For suspending our own Legislatures, and declaring themselves invested with power to legislate for us in all cases whatsoever.

He has abdicated Government here, by declaring us out of his Protection and waging War against us.

He has plundered our seas, ravaged our coasts, burnt our towns, and destroyed the lives of our people.

He is at this time transporting large Armies of foreign Mercenaries to compleat the works of death, desolation, and tyranny, already begun with circumstances of Cruelty & Perfidy scarcely paralleled in the most barbarous ages, and totally unworthy the Head of a civilized nation.

He has constrained our fellow Citizens taken Captive on the high Seas to bear Arms against their Country, to become the executioners of their friends and Brethren, or to fall themselves by their Hands.

He has excited domestic insurrections amongst us, and has endeavoured to bring on the inhabitants of our frontiers, the merciless Indian Savages whose known rule of warfare, is an undistinguished destruction of all ages, sexes and conditions.

In every stage of these Oppressions We have Petitioned for Redress in the most humble terms: Our repeated Petitions have been answered only by repeated injury. A Prince, whose character is thus marked by every act which may define a Tyrant, is unfit to be the ruler of a free people.

Nor have We been wanting in attentions to our British brethren. We have warned them from time to time of attempts by their legislature to extend an unwarrantable jurisdiction over us. We have reminded them of the circumstances of our emigration and settlement here. We have appealed to their native justice and magnanimity, and we have conjured them by the ties of our common kindred to disavow these usurpations, which would inevitably interrupt our connections and correspondence. They too have been deaf to the voice of justice and of consanguinity. We must, therefore, acquiesce in the necessity, which denounces our Separation, and hold them, as we hold the rest of mankind, Enemies in War, in Peace Friends.

We, therefore, the Representatives of the united States of America, in General Congress, Assembled, appealing to the Supreme Judge of the world for the rectitude of our intentions, do, in the Name, and by Authority of the good People of these Colonies, solemnly publish and declare, That these united Colonies are, and of Right ought to be Free and Independent States, that they are Absolved from all Allegiance to the British Crown, and that all political connection between them and the State of Great Britain, is and ought to be totally dissolved; and that as Free and Independent States, they have full Power to levy War, conclude Peace, contract Alliances, establish Commerce, and to do all other Acts and Things which Independent States may of right do. — And for the support of this Declaration, with a firm reliance on the protection of Divine Providence, we mutually pledge to each other our Lives, our Fortunes, and our sacred Honor.

New Hampshire:

Josiah Bartlett, William Whipple, Matthew Thornton

Massachusetts:

John Hancock, Samuel Adams, John Adams, Robert Treat Paine, Elbridge Gerry

Rhode Island:

Stephen Hopkins, William Ellery

Connecticut:

Roger Sherman, Samuel Huntington, William Williams, Oliver Wolcott

New York:

William Floyd, Philip Livingston, Francis Lewis, Lewis Morris

New Jersey:

Richard Stockton, John Witherspoon, Francis Hopkinson, John Hart, Abraham Clark

Pennsylvania:

Robert Morris, Benjamin Rush, Benjamin Franklin, John Morton, George Clymer, James Smith, George Taylor, James Wilson, George Ross

Delaware:

Caesar Rodney, George Read, Thomas McKean

Maryland:

Samuel Chase, William Paca, Thomas Stone, Charles Carroll of Carrollton

Virginia:

George Wythe, Richard Henry Lee, Thomas Jefferson, Benjamin Harrison, Thomas Nelson, Jr., Francis Lightfoot Lee, Carter Braxton

North Carolina:

William Hooper, Joseph Hewes, John Penn

South Carolina:

Edward Rutledge, Thomas Heyward, Jr., Thomas Lynch, Jr., Arthur Middleton

Georgia:

Button Gwinnett, Lyman Hall, George Walton

The Constitution of the United States

The Complete Text with Original Spelling and Capitalization

We the People of the United States, in Order to form a more perfect Union, establish Justice, insure domestic Tranquility, provide for the common defence, promote the general Welfare, and secure the Blessings of Liberty to ourselves and our Posterity, do ordain and establish this Constitution for the United States of America.

Article I

Section 1. All legislative Powers herein granted shall be vested in a Congress of the United States, which shall consist of a Senate and House of Representatives.

Section 2. The House of Representatives shall be composed of Members chosen every second Year by the People of the several States, and the Electors in each State shall have the Qualifications requisite for Electors of the most numerous Branch of the State Legislature.

No person shall be a Representative who shall not have attained to the age of twenty five Years, and been seven Years a Citizen of the United States, and who shall not, when elected, be an Inhabitant of that State in which he shall be chosen.

Representatives and direct Taxes shall be apportioned among the several States which may be included within this Union, according to their respective Numbers, which shall be determined by adding to the whole Number of free Persons, including those bound to Service for a Term of Years, and excluding Indians not taxed, three fifths of all other Persons.

The actual Enumeration shall be made within three Years after the first Meeting of the Congress of the United States, and within every subsequent Term of ten Years, in such Manner as they shall by Law direct. The Number of Representatives shall not exceed one for every thirty Thousand, but each State shall have at Least one Representative; and until such enumeration shall be made, the State of New Hampshire shall be entitled to chuse three, Massachusetts eight, Rhode-Island and Providence Plantations one, Connecticut five, New-York six, New Jersey four, Pennsylvania eight, Delaware one, Maryland six, Virginia ten, North Carolina five, South Carolina five, and Georgia three.

When vacancies happen in the Representation from any State, the Executive Authority thereof shall issue Writs of Election to fill such Vacancies.

The House of Representatives shall chuse their Speaker and other Officers; and shall have the sole Power of Impeachment.

Section 3. The Senate of the United States shall be composed of two Senators from each State, chosen by the Legislature thereof, for six Years; and each Senator shall have one Vote.

Immediately after they shall be assembled in Consequence of the first Election, they shall be divided as equally as may be into three Classes. The Seats of the Senators of the first Class shall be vacated at the Expiration of the second Year, of the second Class at the Expiration of the fourth Year, and the third Class at the Expiration of the sixth Year, so that one third may be chosen every second Year; and if Vacancies happen by Resignation, or otherwise, during the Recess of the Legislature of any State, the Executive thereof may make temporary Appointments until the next Meeting of the Legislature, which shall then fill such Vacancies.

No Person shall be a Senator who shall not have attained to the Age of thirty Years, and been nine Years a Citizen of the

United States and who shall not, when elected, be an Inhabitant of that State for which he shall be chosen.

The Vice President of the United States shall be President of the Senate, but shall have no Vote, unless they be equally divided.

The Senate shall chuse their other Officers, and also a President pro tempore, in the Absence of the Vice President, or when he shall exercise the Office of President of the United States.

The Senate shall have the sole Power to try all Impeachments. When sitting for that Purpose, they shall be on Oath or Affirmation. When the President of the United States is tried, the Chief Justice shall preside: And no Person shall be convicted without the Concurrence of two thirds of the Members present.

Judgment in Cases of Impeachment shall not extend further than to removal from Office, and disqualification to hold and enjoy any Office of Honor, Trust or Profit under the United States: but the Party convicted shall nevertheless be liable and subject to Indictment, Trial, Judgment and Punishment, according to Law.

Section 4. The Times, Places and Manner of holding Elections for Senators and Representatives, shall be prescribed in each State by the Legislature thereof; but the Congress may at any time by Law make or alter such Regulations, except as to the Places of chusing Senators.

The Congress shall assemble at least once in every Year, and such Meeting shall be on the first Monday in December, unless they shall by Law appoint a different Day.

Section 5. Each House shall be the Judge of the Elections, Returns and Qualifications of its own Members, and a Majority of each shall constitute a Quorum to do Business; but a smaller

Number may adjourn from day to day, and may be authorized to compel the Attendance of absent Members, in such Manner, and under such Penalties as each House may provide.

Each House may determine the Rules of its Proceedings, punish its Members for disorderly Behaviour, and, with the Concurrence of two thirds, expel a Member.

Each House shall keep a Journal of its Proceedings, and from time to time publish the same, excepting such Parts as may in their Judgment require Secrecy; and the Yeas and Nays of the Members of either House on any question shall, at the Desire of one fifth of those Present, be entered on the Journal.

Neither House, during the Session of Congress, shall, without the Consent of the other, adjourn for more than three days, nor to any other Place than that in which the two Houses shall be sitting.

Section 6. The Senators and Representatives shall receive a Compensation for their Services, to be ascertained by Law, and paid out of the Treasury of the United States. They shall in all Cases, except Treason, Felony and Breach of the Peace, be privileged from Arrest during their Attendance at the Session of their respective Houses, and in going to and returning from the same; and for any Speech or Debate in either House, they shall not be questioned in any other Place.

No Senator or Representative shall, during the Time for which he was elected, be appointed to any civil Office under the Authority of the United States, which shall have been created, or the Emoluments whereof shall have been encreased during such time: and no Person holding any Office under the United States, shall be a Member of either House during his Continuance in Office.

Section 7. All Bills for raising Revenue shall originate in the House of Representatives; but the Senate may propose or concur with Amendments as on other Bills.

Every Bill which shall have passed the House of Representatives and the Senate, shall, before it become a Law, be presented to the President of the United States; if he approve he shall sign it, but if not he shall return it, with his Objections to that House in which it shall have originated, who shall enter the Objections at large on their Journal, and proceed to reconsider it. If after such Reconsideration two thirds of that House shall agree to pass the Bill, it shall be sent, together with the Objections, to the other House, by which it shall likewise be reconsidered, and if approved by two thirds of that House, it shall become a Law. But in all such Cases the Votes of both Houses shall be determined by Yeas and Nays, and the Names of the Persons voting for and against the Bill shall be entered on the Journal of each House respectively. If any Bill shall not be returned by the President within ten Days (Sundays excepted) after it shall have been presented to him, the Same shall be a Law, in like Manner as if he had signed it, unless the Congress by their Adjournment prevent its Return, in which Case it shall not be a Law.

Every Order, Resolution, or Vote to which the Concurrence of the Senate and House of Representatives may be necessary (except on a question of Adjournment) shall be presented to the President of the United States; and before the Same shall take Effect, shall be approved by him, or being disapproved by him, shall be repassed by two thirds of the Senate and House of Representatives, according to the Rules and Limitations prescribed in the Case of a Bill.

Section 8. The Congress shall have Power To lay and collect Taxes, Duties, Imposts and Excises, to pay the Debts and provide for the common Defence and general Welfare of the United States; but all Duties, Imposts and Excises shall be uniform throughout the United States;

To borrow Money on the credit of the United States;

To regulate Commerce with foreign Nations, and among the several States, and with the Indian Tribes;

To establish an uniform Rule of Naturalization, and uniform Laws on the subject of Bankruptcies throughout the United States;

To coin Money, regulate the Value thereof, and of foreign Coin, and fix the Standard of Weights and Measures;

To provide for the Punishment of counterfeiting the Securities and current Coin of the United States;

To establish Post Offices and post Roads;

To promote the Progress of Science and useful Arts, by securing for limited Times to Authors and Inventors the exclusive Right to their respective Writings and Discoveries;

To constitute Tribunals inferior to the supreme Court;

To define and punish Piracies and Felonies committed on the high Seas, and Offences against the Law of Nations;

To declare War, grant Letters of Marque and Reprisal, and make Rules concerning Captures on Land and Water;

To raise and support Armies, but no Appropriation of Money to that Use shall be for a longer Term than two Years;

To provide and maintain a Navy;

To make Rules for the Government and Regulation of the land and naval Forces;

To provide for calling forth the Militia to execute the Laws of the Union, suppress Insurrections and repel Invasions;

To provide for organizing, arming, and disciplining, the Militia, and for governing such Part of them as may be employed in the Service of the United States, reserving to the States respectively, the Appointment of the Officers, and the

Authority of training the Militia according to the discipline prescribed by Congress;

To exercise exclusive Legislation in all Cases whatsoever, over such District (not exceeding ten Miles square) as may, by Cession of particular States, and the Acceptance of Congress, become the Seat of the Government of the United States, and to exercise like Authority over all Places purchased by the Consent of the Legislature of the State in which the Same shall be, for the Erection of Forts, Magazines, Arsenals, dock-Yards, and other needful Buildings;--And

To make all Laws which shall be necessary and proper for carrying into Execution the foregoing Powers, and all other Powers vested by this Constitution in the Government of the United States, or in any Department or Officer thereof.

Section 9. The Migration or Importation of such Persons as any of the States now existing shall think proper to admit, shall not be prohibited by the Congress prior to the Year one thousand eight hundred and eight, but a Tax or duty may be imposed on such Importation, not exceeding ten dollars for each Person.

The Privilege of the Writ of Habeas Corpus shall not be suspended, unless when in Cases of Rebellion or Invasion the public Safety may require it.

No Bill of Attainder or ex post facto Law shall be passed.

No Capitation, or other direct, Tax shall be laid, unless in Proportion to the Census or Enumeration herein before directed to be taken.

No Tax or Duty shall be laid on Articles exported from any State.

No Preference shall be given by any Regulation of Commerce or Revenue to the Ports of one State over those of another: nor shall Vessels bound to, or from, one State, be obliged to enter, clear or pay Duties in another.

No Money shall be drawn from the Treasury, but in Consequence of Appropriations made by Law; and a regular Statement and Account of Receipts and Expenditures of all public Money shall be published from time to time.

No Title of Nobility shall be granted by the United States: And no Person holding any Office of Profit or Trust under them, shall, without the Consent of the Congress, accept of any present, Emolument, Office, or Title, of any kind whatever, from any King, Prince, or foreign State.

Section 10. No State shall enter into any Treaty, Alliance, or Confederation; grant Letters of Marque and Reprisal; coin Money; emit Bills of Credit; make any Thing but gold and silver Coin a Tender in Payment of Debts; pass any Bill of Attainder, ex post facto Law, or Law impairing the Obligation of Contracts, or grant any Title of Nobility.

No State shall, without the Consent of the Congress, lay any Imposts or Duties on Imports or Exports, except what may be absolutely necessary for executing it's inspection Laws: and the net Produce of all Duties and Imposts, laid by any State on Imports or Exports, shall be for the Use of the Treasury of the United States; and all such Laws shall be subject to the Revision and Controul of the Congress.

No State shall, without the Consent of Congress, lay any Duty of Tonnage, keep Troops, or Ships of War in time of Peace, enter into any Agreement or Compact with another State, or with a foreign Power, or engage in War, unless actually invaded, or in such imminent Danger as will not admit of delay.

Article II

Section 1. The executive Power shall be vested in a President of the United States of America. He shall hold his Office during the Term of four Years, and, together with the Vice President, chosen for the same Term, be elected, as follows:

Each State shall appoint, in such Manner as the Legislature thereof may direct, a Number of Electors, equal to the whole Number of Senators and Representatives to which the State may be entitled in the Congress: but no Senator or Representative, or Person holding an Office of Trust or Profit under the United States, shall be appointed an Elector.

The Electors shall meet in their respective States, and vote by Ballot for two Persons, of whom one at least shall not be an Inhabitant of the same State with themselves. And they shall make a List of all the Persons voted for, and of the Number of Votes for each; which List they shall sign and certify, and transmit sealed to the Seat of the Government of the United States, directed to the President of the Senate. The President of the Senate shall, in the Presence of the Senate and House of Representatives, open all the Certificates, and the Votes shall then be counted. The Person having the greatest Number of Votes shall be the President, if such Number be a Majority of the whole Number of Electors appointed; and if there be more than one who have such Majority, and have an equal Number of Votes, then the House of Representatives shall immediately chuse by Ballot one of them for President; and if no Person have a Majority, then from the five highest on the List the said House shall in like Manner chuse the President. But in chusing the President, the Votes shall be taken by States, the Representation from each State having one Vote; A quorum for this Purpose shall consist of a Member or Members from two thirds of the States, and a Majority of all the States shall be necessary to a Choice. In every Case, after the Choice of the President, the Person having the greatest Number of Votes of the Electors shall be the Vice President. But if there should remain two or more who have equal Votes, the Senate shall chuse from them by Ballot the Vice President.

The Congress may determine the Time of chusing the Electors, and the Day on which they shall give their Votes; which Day shall be the same throughout the United States.

No Person except a natural born Citizen, or a Citizen of the United States, at the time of the Adoption of this Constitution, shall be eligible to the Office of President; neither shall any Person be eligible to that Office who shall not have attained to the Age of thirty five Years, and been fourteen Years a Resident within the United States.

In Case of the Removal of the President from Office, or of his Death, Resignation, or Inability to discharge the Powers and Duties of the said Office, the Same shall devolve on the Vice President, and the Congress may by Law provide for the Case of Removal, Death, Resignation or Inability, both of the President and Vice President, declaring what Officer shall then act as President, and such Officer shall act accordingly, until the Disability be removed, or a President shall be elected.

The President shall, at stated Times, receive for his Services, a Compensation, which shall neither be encreased nor diminished during the Period for which he shall have been elected, and he shall not receive within that Period any other Emolument from the United States, or any of them.

Before he enter on the Execution of his Office, he shall take the following Oath or Affirmation:--"I do solemnly swear (or affirm) that I will faithfully execute the Office of President of the United States, and will to the best of my Ability, preserve, protect and defend the Constitution of the United States."

Section 2. The President shall be Commander in Chief of the Army and Navy of the United States, and of the Militia of the several States, when called into the actual Service of the United States; he may require the Opinion, in writing, of the principal Officer in each of the executive Departments, upon any Subject relating to the Duties of their respective Offices, and he shall have Power to grant Reprieves and Pardons for Offences against the United States, except in Cases of Impeachment.

He shall have Power, by and with the Advice and Consent of the Senate, to make Treaties, provided two thirds of the Senators present concur; and he shall nominate, and by and with the Advice and Consent of the Senate, shall appoint Ambassadors, other public Ministers and Consuls, Judges of the supreme Court, and all other Officers of the United States, whose Appointments are not herein otherwise provided for, and which shall be established by Law: but the Congress may by Law vest the Appointment of such inferior Officers, as they think proper, in the President alone, in the Courts of Law, or in the Heads of Departments.

The President shall have Power to fill up all Vacancies that may happen during the Recess of the Senate, by granting Commissions which shall expire at the End of their next Session.

Section 3. He shall from time to time give to the Congress Information of the State of the Union, and recommend to their Consideration such Measures as he shall judge necessary and expedient; he may, on extraordinary Occasions, convene both Houses, or either of them, and in Case of Disagreement between them, with Respect to the Time of Adjournment, he may adjourn them to such Time as he shall think proper; he shall receive Ambassadors and other public Ministers; he shall take Care that the Laws be faithfully executed, and shall Commission all the Officers of the United States.

Section 4. The President, Vice President and all civil Officers of the United States, shall be removed from Office on Impeachment for, and Conviction of, Treason, Bribery, or other high Crimes and Misdemeanors.

Article III

Section 1. The judicial Power of the United States, shall be vested in one supreme Court, and in such inferior Courts as the Congress may from time to time ordain and establish. The Judges, both of the supreme and inferior Courts, shall hold their Offices during good Behaviour, and shall, at stated Times, receive for their Services, a Compensation, which shall not be diminished during their Continuance in Office.

Section 2. The judicial Power shall extend to all Cases, in Law and Equity, arising under this Constitution, the Laws of the United States, and Treaties made, or which shall be made, under their Authority;--to all Cases affecting Ambassadors, other public Ministers and Consuls;--to all Cases of admiralty and maritime Jurisdiction;--to Controversies to which the United States shall be a Party;--to Controversies between two or more States;--between a State and Citizens of another State;--between Citizens of different States;--between Citizens of the same State claiming Lands under Grants of different States, and between a State, or the Citizens thereof, and foreign States, Citizens or Subjects.

In all Cases affecting Ambassadors, other public Ministers and Consuls, and those in which a State shall be Party, the supreme Court shall have original Jurisdiction. In all the other Cases before mentioned, the supreme Court shall have appellate Jurisdiction, both as to Law and Fact, with such Exceptions, and under such Regulations as the Congress shall make.

The Trial of all Crimes, except in Cases of Impeachment, shall be by Jury; and such Trial shall be held in the State where the said Crimes shall have been committed; but when not committed within any State, the Trial shall be at such Place or Places as the Congress may by Law have directed.

Section 3. Treason against the United States, shall consist only in levying War against them, or in adhering to their Enemies, giving them Aid and Comfort. No Person shall be convicted of

Treason unless on the Testimony of two Witnesses to the same overt Act, or on Confession in open Court.

The Congress shall have Power to declare the Punishment of Treason, but no Attainder of Treason shall work Corruption of Blood, or Forfeiture except during the Life of the Person attainted.

Article IV

Section 1. Full Faith and Credit shall be given in each State to the public Acts, Records, and judicial Proceedings of every other State. And the Congress may by general Laws prescribe the Manner in which such Acts, Records, and Proceedings shall be proved, and the Effect thereof.

Section 2. The Citizens of each State shall be entitled to all Privileges and Immunities of Citizens in the several States.

A Person charged in any State with Treason, Felony, or other Crime, who shall flee from Justice, and be found in another State, shall on Demand of the executive Authority of the State from which he fled, be delivered up, to be removed to the State having Jurisdiction of the Crime.

No Person held to Service or Labour in one State, under the Laws thereof, escaping into another, shall, in Consequence of any Law or Regulation therein, be discharged from such Service or Labour, but shall be delivered up on Claim of the Party to whom such Service or Labour may be due.

Section 3. New States may be admitted by the Congress into this Union; but no new States shall be formed or erected within the Jurisdiction of any other State; nor any State be formed by the Junction of two or more States, or Parts of States, without the Consent of the Legislatures of the States concerned as well as of the Congress.

The Congress shall have Power to dispose of and make all needful Rules and Regulations respecting the Territory or other

Property belonging to the United States; and nothing in this Constitution shall be so construed as to Prejudice any Claims of the United States, or of any particular State.

Section 4. The United States shall guarantee to every State in this Union a Republican Form of Government, and shall protect each of them against Invasion; and on Application of the Legislature, or of the Executive (when the Legislature cannot be convened) against domestic Violence.

Article V

The Congress, whenever two thirds of both Houses shall deem it necessary, shall propose Amendments to this Constitution, or, on the Application of the Legislatures of two thirds of the several States, shall call a Convention for proposing Amendments, which, in either Case, shall be valid to all Intents and Purposes, as Part of this Constitution, when ratified by the Legislatures of three fourths of the several States, or by Conventions in three fourths thereof, as the one or the other Mode of Ratification may be proposed by the Congress; Provided that no Amendment which may be made prior to the Year One thousand eight hundred and eight shall in any Manner affect the first and fourth Clauses in the Ninth Section of the first Article; and that no State, without its Consent, shall be deprived of its equal Suffrage in the Senate.

Article VI

All Debts contracted and Engagements entered into, before the Adoption of this Constitution, shall be as valid against the United States under this Constitution, as under the Confederation.

This Constitution, and the Laws of the United States which shall be made in Pursuance thereof; and all Treaties made, or which shall be made, under the Authority of the United States, shall be the supreme Law of the Land; and the Judges in every

State shall be bound thereby, any Thing in the Constitution or Laws of any State to the Contrary notwith-standing.

The Senators and Representatives before mentioned, and the Members of the several State Legislatures, and all executive and judicial Officers, both of the United States and of the several States, shall be bound by Oath or Affirmation, to support this Constitution; but no religious Test shall ever be required as a Qualification to any Office or public Trust under the United States.

Article VII

The Ratification of the Conventions of nine States, shall be sufficient for the Establishment of this Constitution between the States so ratifying the Same.

Done in Convention by the Unanimous Consent of the States present the Seventeenth Day of September in the Year of our Lord one thousand seven hundred and Eighty seven and of the Independence of the United States of America the Twelfth

In witness whereof We have hereunto subscribed our Names,

George Washington--President and deputy from Virginia

New Hampshire: John Langdon, Nicholas Gilman

Massachusetts: Nathaniel Gorham, Rufus King

Connecticut: William Samuel Johnson, Roger Sherman

New York: Alexander Hamilton

New Jersey: William Livingston, David Brearly, William Paterson, Jonathan Dayton

Pennsylvania: Benjamin Franklin, Thomas Mifflin, Robert Morris, George Clymer, Thomas FitzSimons, Jared Ingersoll, James Wilson, Gouverneur Morris

Delaware: George Read, Gunning Bedford, Jr., John Dickinson, Richard Bassett, Jacob Broom

Maryland: James McHenry, Daniel of Saint Thomas Jenifer, Daniel Carroll

Virginia: John Blair, James Madison, Jr.

North Carolina: William Blount, Richard Dobbs Spaight, Hugh Williamson

South Carolina: John Rutledge, Charles Cotesworth Pinckney, Charles Pinckney, Pierce Butler

Georgia: William Few, Abraham Baldwin

Addendum: Important dates in U.S. Constitutional history:

May 14, 1787: The Constitutional Convention begins.

September 17, 1787: The Constitution is adopted by the convention delegates; The Constitutional Convention adjourns.

September 28, 1787: The Congress agrees to send the Constitution to the states for debate and ratification.

December 7, 1787: Delaware ratifies. Vote: 30 for, 0 against.

December 12, 1787: Pennsylvania ratifies. Vote: 46 for, 23 against.

December 18, 1787: New Jersey ratifies. Vote: 38 for, 0 against.

January 2, 1788: Georgia ratifies. Vote: 26 for, 0 against.

January 9, 1788: Connecticut ratifies. Vote: 128 for, 40 against.

February 6, 1788: Massachusetts ratifies. Vote: 187 for, 168 against.

March 24, 1788: Rhode Island popular referendum rejects. Vote: 237 for, 2708 against.

April 28, 1788: Maryland ratifies. Vote: 63 for, 11 against.

May 23, 1788: South Carolina ratifies. Vote: 149 for, 73 against.

June 21, 1788: New Hampshire ratifies. Vote: 57 for, 47 against. Minimum requirement for ratification met.

June 25, 1788: Virginia ratifies. Vote: 89 for, 79 against.

July 26, 1788: New York ratifies. Vote: 30 for, 27 against.

August 2, 1788: North Carolina convention adjourns without ratifying by a vote of 185 in favor of adjournment, 84 opposed.

September 13, 1788: The Constitution is certified.

March 4, 1789: The new government begins operations in New York.

September 25, 1789: Bill of Rights, as promised by supporters of the Constitution, proposed by Congress.

November 21, 1789: North Carolina ratifies. Vote: 194 for, 77 against.

May 29, 1790: Rhode Island ratifies. Vote: 34 for, 32 against.

December 15, 1791: Bill of Rights come into effect through ratification of 3/4 of the states.

The Bill of Rights and Amendments to the U.S. Constitution

There have been a total of 27 amendments to the Constitution. The first ten amendments collectively are known as the Bill of Rights. They were ratified together on December 15, 1791. For all subsequent amendments, the ratification date is listed along with the amendment number:

Amendment I

Congress shall make no law respecting an establishment of religion, or prohibiting the free exercise thereof; or abridging the freedom of speech, or of the press; or the right of the people peaceably to assemble, and to petition the Government for a redress of grievances.

Amendment II

A well regulated Militia, being necessary to the security of a free State, the right of the people to keep and bear Arms, shall not be infringed.

Amendment III

No Soldier shall, in time of peace be quartered in any house, without the consent of the Owner, nor in time of war, but in a manner to be prescribed by law.

Amendment IV

The right of the people to be secure in their persons, houses, papers, and effects, against unreasonable searches and seizures, shall not be violated, and no Warrants shall issue, but upon probable cause, supported by Oath or affirmation, and particularly describing the place to be searched, and the persons or things to be seized.

Amendment V

No person shall be held to answer for a capital, or otherwise infamous crime, unless on a presentment or indictment of a Grand Jury, except in cases arising in the land or naval forces, or in the Militia, when in actual service in time of War or public danger; nor shall any person be subject for the same offence to be twice put in jeopardy of life or limb; nor shall be compelled in any criminal case to be a witness against himself, nor be deprived of life, liberty, or property, without due process of law; nor shall private property be taken for public use, without just compensation.

Amendment VI

In all criminal prosecutions, the accused shall enjoy the right to a speedy and public trial, by an impartial jury of the State and district wherein the crime shall have been committed, which district shall have been previously ascertained by law, and to be informed of the nature and cause of the accusation; to be confronted with the witnesses against him; to have compulsory process for obtaining witnesses in his favor, and to have the Assistance of Counsel for his defence.

Amendment VII

In Suits at common law, where the value in controversy shall exceed twenty dollars, the right of trial by jury shall be preserved, and no fact tried by a jury, shall be otherwise re-examined in any Court of the United States, than according to the rules of the common law.

Amendment VIII

Excessive bail shall not be required, nor excessive fines imposed, nor cruel and unusual punishments inflicted.

Amendment IX

The enumeration in the Constitution, of certain rights, shall not be construed to deny or disparage others retained by the people.

Amendment X

The powers not delegated to the United States by the Constitution, nor prohibited by it to the States, are reserved to the States respectively, or to the people.

Amendment XI (Ratified February 7, 1795)

The Judicial power of the United States shall not be construed to extend to any suit in law or equity, commenced or prosecuted against one of the United States by Citizens of another State, or by Citizens or Subjects of any Foreign State.

Amendment XII (Ratified June 15, 1804)

The Electors shall meet in their respective states, and vote by ballot for President and Vice-President, one of whom, at least, shall not be an inhabitant of the same state with themselves; they shall name in their ballots the person voted for as President, and in distinct ballots the person voted for as Vice-President, and they shall make distinct lists of all persons voted for as President, and of all persons voted for as Vice-President and of the number of votes for each, which lists they shall sign and certify, and transmit sealed to the seat of the government of the United States, directed to the President of the Senate;

The President of the Senate shall, in the presence of the Senate and House of Representatives, open all the certificates and the votes shall then be counted.

The person having the greatest Number of votes for President, shall be the President, if such number be a majority of the whole number of Electors appointed; and if no person have such majority, then from the persons having the highest numbers not exceeding three on the list of those voted for as President, the House of Representatives shall choose immediately, by ballot, the President. But in choosing the President, the votes shall be taken by states, the representation from each state having one vote; a quorum for this purpose shall consist of a member or members from two-thirds of the states, and a majority of all the states shall be necessary to a choice. And if the House of Representatives shall not choose a President whenever the right of choice shall devolve upon them, before the fourth day of March next following, then the Vice-President shall act as President, as in the case of the death or other constitutional disability of the President.

The person having the greatest number of votes as Vice-President, shall be the Vice-President, if such number be a majority of the whole number of Electors appointed, and if no person have a majority, then from the two highest numbers on the list, the Senate shall choose the Vice-President; a quorum for the purpose shall consist of two-thirds of the whole number of Senators, and a majority of the whole number shall be necessary to a choice. But no person constitutionally ineligible to the office of President shall be eligible to that of Vice-President of the United States.

Amendment XIII (Ratified December 6, 1865)

1. Neither slavery nor involuntary servitude, except as a punishment for crime whereof the party shall have been duly convicted, shall exist within the United States, or any place subject to their jurisdiction.

2. Congress shall have power to enforce this article by appropriate legislation.

Amendment XIV (Ratified July 9, 1868)

Section 1

All persons born or naturalized in the United States, and subject to the jurisdiction thereof, are citizens of the United States and of the State wherein they reside. No State shall make or enforce any law which shall abridge the privileges or immunities of citizens of the United States; nor shall any State deprive any person of life, liberty, or property, without due process of law; nor deny to any person within its jurisdiction the equal protection of the laws.

Section 2

Representatives shall be apportioned among the several States according to their respective numbers counting the whole number of persons in each State, excluding Indians not taxed. But when the right to vote at any election for the choice of electors for President and Vice-President of the United States, Representatives in Congress, the Executive and Judicial officers of a State, or the members of the Legislature thereof, is denied to any of the male inhabitants of such State, being twenty-one years of age, and citizens of the United States, or in any way abridged, except for participation in rebellion, or other crime, the basis of representation therein shall be reduced in the proportion which the number of such male citizens shall bear to the whole number of male citizens twenty-one years of age in such State.

Section 3

No person shall be a Senator or Representative in Congress, or elector of President and Vice-President, or hold any office, civil or military, under the United States, or under any State, who, having previously taken an oath, as a member of Congress, or as an officer of the United States, or as a member of any State legislature, or as an executive or judicial officer of any State, to support the Constitution of the United States, shall have engaged in insurrection or rebellion against the same, or given aid or comfort to the enemies thereof. But Congress may by a vote of two-thirds of each House, remove such disability.

Section 4

The validity of the public debt of the United States, authorized by law, including debts incurred for payment of pensions and bounties for services in suppressing insurrection or rebellion, shall not be questioned. But neither the United States nor any State shall assume or pay any debt or obligation incurred in aid of insurrection or rebellion against the United States, or any claim for the loss or emancipation of any slave. But all such debts, obligations and claims shall be held illegal and void.

Section 5

The Congress shall have power to enforce, by appropriate legislation, the provisions of this article.

Amendment XV (Ratified February 3, 1870)

Section 1

The right of citizens of the United States to vote shall not be denied or abridged by the United States or by any State on account of race, color, or previous condition of servitude.

Section 2

The Congress shall have power to enforce this article by appropriate legislation.

Amendment XVI (Ratified February 3, 1913)

The Congress shall have power to lay and collect taxes on incomes, from whatever source derived, without apportionment among the several States, and without regard to any census or enumeration.

Amendment XVII (Ratified April 8, 1913)

The Senate of the United States shall be composed of two Senators from each State, elected by the people thereof, for six years; and each Senator shall have one vote. The electors in each State shall have the qualifications requisite for electors of the most numerous branch of the State legislatures.

When vacancies happen in the representation of any State in the Senate, the executive authority of such State shall issue writs of election to fill such vacancies: Provided, That the legislature of any State may empower the executive thereof to make temporary appointments until the people fill the vacancies by election as the legislature may direct.

This amendment shall not be so construed as to affect the election or term of any Senator chosen before it becomes valid as part of the Constitution.

Amendment XVIII

(Ratified January 16, 1919)

(Repealed December 5, 1933 with the Ratification of Amendment XXI)

Section 1

After one year from the ratification of this article the manufacture, sale, or transportation of intoxicating liquors within, the importation thereof into, or the exportation thereof from the United States and all territory subject to the jurisdiction thereof for beverage purposes is hereby prohibited.

Section 2

The Congress and all of the several States shall have concurrent power to enforce this article by appropriate legislation.

Section 3

This article shall be inoperative unless it shall have been ratified as an amendment to the Constitution by the legislatures of the several States, as provided in the Constitution, within seven years from the date of the submission hereof to the States by the Congress.

Amendment XIX (Ratified August 18, 1920)

The right of citizens of the United States to vote shall not be denied or abridged by the United States or by any State on account of sex.

Congress shall have power to enforce this article by appropriate legislation.

Amendment XX (Ratified January 23, 1933)

Section 1

The terms of the President and Vice President shall end at noon on the 20th day of January, and the terms of Senators and Representatives at noon on the 3d day of January, of the years in which such terms would have ended if this article had not been ratified; and the terms of their successors shall then begin.

Section 2

The Congress shall assemble at least once in every year, and such meeting shall begin at noon on the 3d day of January, unless they shall by law appoint a different day.

Section 3

If, at the time fixed for the beginning of the term of the President, the President elect shall have died, the Vice President elect shall become President. If a President shall not have been chosen before the time fixed for the beginning of his term, or if the President elect shall have failed to qualify, then the Vice President elect shall act as President until a President shall have qualified; and the Congress may by law provide for the case wherein neither a President elect nor a Vice President elect shall have qualified, declaring who shall then act as President, or the manner in which one who is to act shall be selected, and such person shall act accordingly until a President or Vice President shall have qualified.

Section 4

The Congress may by law provide for the case of the death of any of the persons from whom the House of Representatives may choose a President whenever the right of choice shall have devolved upon them, and for the case of the death of any of the persons from whom the Senate may choose a Vice President whenever the right of choice shall have devolved upon them.

Section 5

Sections 1 and 2 shall take effect on the 15th day of October following the ratification of this article.

Section 6

This article shall be inoperative unless it shall have been ratified as an amendment to the Constitution by the legislatures of three-fourths of the several States within seven years from the date of its submission.

Amendment XXI (Ratified December 5, 1933)

Section 1

The eighteenth article of amendment to the Constitution of the United States is hereby repealed.

Section 2

The transportation or importation into any State, Territory, or possession of the United States for delivery or use therein of intoxicating liquors, in violation of the laws thereof, is hereby prohibited.

Section 3

The article shall be inoperative unless it shall have been ratified as an amendment to the Constitution by conventions in the several States, as provided in the Constitution, within seven years from the date of the submission hereof to the States by the Congress.

Amendment XXII (Ratified February 27, 1951)

Section 1

No person shall be elected to the office of the President more than twice, and no person who has held the office of President, or acted as President, for more than two years of a term to which some other person was elected President shall be elected to the office of the President more than once. But this Article shall not apply to any person holding the office of President, when this Article was proposed by the Congress, and shall not prevent any person who may be holding the office of President, or acting as President, during the term within which this Article becomes operative from holding the office of President or acting as President during the remainder of such term.

Section 2

This article shall be inoperative unless it shall have been ratified as an amendment to the Constitution by the legislatures of three-fourths of the several States within seven years from the date of its submission to the States by the Congress.

Amendment XXIII (Ratified March 19, 1961)

Section 1

The District constituting the seat of Government of the United States shall appoint in such manner as the Congress may direct: A number of electors of President and Vice President equal to the whole number of Senators and Representatives in Congress to which the District would be entitled if it were a State, but in no event more than the least populous State; they shall be in addition to those appointed by the States, but they shall be considered, for the purposes of the election of President and Vice President, to be electors appointed by a State; and they shall meet in the District and perform such duties as provided by the twelfth article of amendment.

Section 2

The Congress shall have power to enforce this article by appropriate legislation.

Amendment XXIV (Ratified January 23, 1964)

Section 1

The right of citizens of the United States to vote in any primary or other election for President or Vice President, for electors for President or Vice President, or for Senator or Representative in Congress, shall not be denied or abridged by the United States or any State by reason of failure to pay any poll tax or other tax.

Section 2

The Congress shall have power to enforce this article by appropriate legislation.

Amendment XXV (Ratified February 10, 1967)

Section 1

In case of the removal of the President from office or of his death or resignation, the Vice President shall become President.

Section 2

Whenever there is a vacancy in the office of the Vice President, the President shall nominate a Vice President who shall take office upon confirmation by a majority vote of both Houses of Congress.

Section 3

Whenever the President transmits to the President pro tempore of the Senate and the Speaker of the House of Representatives his written declaration that he is unable to discharge the powers and duties of his office, and until he transmits to them a written declaration to the contrary, such powers and duties shall be discharged by the Vice President as Acting President.

Section 4

Whenever the Vice President and a majority of either the principal officers of the executive departments or of such other body as Congress may by law provide, transmit to the President pro tempore of the Senate and the Speaker of the House of Representatives their written declaration that the President is unable to discharge the powers and duties of his office, the Vice President shall immediately assume the powers and duties of the office as Acting President.

Thereafter, when the President transmits to the President pro tempore of the Senate and the Speaker of the House of Representatives his written declaration that no inability exists, he shall resume the powers and duties of his office unless the Vice President and a majority of either the principal officers of the executive department or of such other body as Congress may by law provide, transmit within four days to the President pro tempore of the Senate and the Speaker of the House of Representatives their written declaration that the President is unable to discharge the powers and duties of his office. Thereupon Congress shall decide the issue, assembling within forty eight hours for that purpose if not in session. If the Congress, within twenty one days after receipt of the latter written declaration, or, if Congress is not in session, within twenty one days after Congress is required to assemble, determines by two thirds vote of both Houses that the President is unable to discharge the powers and duties of his office, the Vice President shall continue to discharge the same as Acting

President; otherwise, the President shall resume the powers and duties of his office.

Amendment XXVI (Ratified July 1, 1971)

The right of citizens of the United States, who are eighteen years of age or older, to vote shall not be denied or abridged by the United States or by any State on account of age. Congress shall have the power to enforce this law through appropriate legislation.

Amendment XXVII (Ratified May 5, 1992)

No law, varying the compensation for the services of the Senators and Representatives, shall take effect, until an election of Representatives shall have intervened.